NATO and the Challenges of Austerity

T0302664

F. Stephen Larrabee, Stuart E. Johnson,
John Gordon IV, Peter A. Wilson, Caroline Baxter,
Deborah Lai, Calin Trenkov-Wermuth

Prepared for the Office of the Secretary of Defense
Approved for public release; distribution unlimited

RAND NATIONAL DEFENSE RESEARCH INSTITUTE

The research described in this report was prepared for the Office of the Secretary of Defense (OSD). The research was conducted within the RAND National Defense Research Institute, a federally funded research and development center sponsored by OSD, the Joint Staff, the Unified Combatant Commands, the Navy, the Marine Corps, the defense agencies, and the defense Intelligence Community under Contract W74V8H-06-C-0002.

Library of Congress Cataloging-in-Publication Data is available for this publication.

ISBN: 978-0-8330-6847-7

Cover photo by NATO: Nation flags outside a summit meeting in Baden-Baden.

Published 2012 by the RAND Corporation
1776 Main Street, P.O. Box 2138, Santa Monica, CA 90407-2138
1200 South Hayes Street, Arlington, VA 22202-5050
4570 Fifth Avenue, Suite 600, Pittsburgh, PA 15213-2665
RAND URL: http://www.rand.org/
To order RAND documents or to obtain additional information, contact
Distribution Services: Telephone: (310) 451-7002;
Fax: (310) 451-6915; Email: order@rand.org

Preface

Financial and economic constraints are redefining NATO's ability to provide security in the coming decade. While the fact that the European members of NATO face pressures to make serious defense cuts is widely recognized in Alliance capitals, the discussion to date has tended to underestimate the magnitude of the cuts on NATO capabilities and their long-term strategic impact. NATO faces more than a simple, short-term budget squeeze: It is confronted with a secular trend that will have a serious impact on NATO Europe's ability to deploy and sustain military power.

At the same time, the United States is facing strong fiscal pressures on defense spending while giving greater priority to the Indo-Pacific region and trimming its military posture in Europe. The totality of these measures will have a major short- and medium-term impact on the overall military health of the Atlantic alliance.

This study analyzes the impact of planned defense budget cuts on the capabilities of seven European members of NATO: the United Kingdom, France, Germany, Italy, Spain, the Netherlands, and Poland. These seven countries were selected because they have the highest proportion of deployable and sustainable forces. Together they represent somewhat more than 80 percent of NATO Europe's defense spending.

This research was sponsored by the office of NATO and European Policy in the Office of the Secretary of Defense and conducted within the International Security and Defense Policy Center of the RAND National Defense Research Institute, a federally funded research and development center sponsored by the Office of the Secretary of Defense, the Joint Staff, the Unified Combatant Commands, the Navy, the Marine Corps, the defense agencies, and the defense Intelligence Community.

For more information on the International Security and Defense Policy Center, see http://www.rand.org/nsrd/ndri/centers/isdp.html or contact the director (contact information is provided on the web page).

Contents

Figures

Summary

In the coming decade, NATO faces growing fiscal austerity and declining defense budgets. The global economic crisis has forced most European governments to trim their defense budgets: Germany will reduce defense spending by a quarter over the next four years, Britain's defense budget will be slashed by more than 8 percent in real terms by 2015, and the defense budgets of some of the smaller European nations have taken even larger cuts. The United States is also planning significant reductions.

These cuts have been driven almost entirely by the need to reduce large budget deficits—not by a change in the nature of external threats. The cuts have been made, moreover, with little intra-Alliance coordination. If this uncoordinated process of budget cuts and reductions intensifies, NATO will lose critical capabilities. U.S. and European forces might no longer be able to operate together to meet evolving security challenges confronting the Alliance.

Meanwhile, the United States is shifting defense priorities. The Obama administration's national security strategy, released in January 2012, gives increased priority to U.S. engagement in Asia and the Pacific.[1] As Washington focuses increasing attention on enhancing stability and security in Asia, pressure is likely to grow on America's European allies to take greater responsibility for providing security in areas such as the Mediterranean littoral, where Europe has strong historical interests. The planned cuts, however, will greatly limit NATO Europe's ability to assume any such responsibility.

---

[1] "Sustaining U.S. Global Leadership: Priorities for 21st Century Defense," U.S. Department of Defense, January 2012.

Impact of Planned Cuts on the Capabilities of Key NATO Members

The impact of planned cuts on the armed forces of seven key allies—the United Kingdom, France, Germany, Italy, Spain, the Netherlands, and Poland—is summarized below. These seven countries were selected because they have the highest proportion of deployable and sustainable forces. Together they represent somewhat more than 80 percent of NATO Europe's defense spending.

The United Kingdom

The current UK government is undertaking a draconian downsizing of the British Armed Forces. All three major services will face significant reductions. The Royal Navy has demobilized its naval combat air fleet with the hope that a new generation of capability will emerge by the end of this decade. The British Army is being reduced in size to that of its pre–Boer War Victorian counterpart and will become a heavyweight force equipped with a modest number of armored fighting vehicles (AFVs). In 2010, the British Army had roughly 100,000 troops in the active force. Under the most recent British plans, by 2018 the army will decline to about 82,000 active duty personnel.[2] In turn, the Royal Air Force (RAF) will shrink in size to the equivalent of five U.S. Air Force (USAF) air combat squadrons (approximately 130 Typhoon fighter bombers). Furthermore, much of the RAF's airborne intelligence, surveillance, and reconnaissance (ISR) capability is on track to being demobilized. If the RAF does not buy the F-35B, its resulting total inventory of 132 Typhoons by the end of the decade will mean that the RAF will be smaller than the air force of Singapore.

Although the Franco-UK Defense Treaty appears promising in a number of dimensions, these areas of cooperation will be hostage to the UK's ability to undertake three major procurement programs during the beginning of the next decade: (1) acquisition of a naval fighter fleet to populate the *Queen Elizabeth*–class aircraft carriers, (2) the mod-

[2] "Army 2020: Presentation to the Army Chain of Command 5 July 2012," Secretary of State A2020 announcement, UK Ministry of Defence, 2012.

ernization of the British Army's AFV fleet, and (3) the investment in a follow-on to the *Vanguard*-class ballistic missile submarine (SSBN) fleet to assure a continuous at-sea deterrent posture.

France

France is more militarily engaged in NATO now than at any time since the 1960s, fielding sizable ground and air forces in Afghanistan and its aircraft carrier in NATO operations in Libya 2011. France intends to maintain a credible "full-spectrum" capability despite cuts to its military. As it has done in the past when facing budgetary austerity, Paris will seek to protect its major weapon system programs by stretching its procurement out even at the cost of production inefficiencies and higher unit costs. The new Hollande government plans a strategic review of France's national military strategy, which may call for further defense reductions above and beyond those proposed by the previous Sarkozy administration. Given the current budget pressure facing the new French government, further defense spending cuts are likely.

The French military has been stretched dangerously thin by recent engagements. The aircraft carrier *Charles de Gaulle* that France sent to support operations in Libya is the sole carrier in France's arsenal, and maintenance needs restrict the amount it can be used. The 2008 French White Paper on Defence and National Security called for reductions in the overall number of French troops, from 270,000 to 225,000, and corresponding budget cuts. Therefore, though France may be a most willing partner, its capabilities will be limited.

Germany

Germany also faces deep cuts in its armed forces. The German Ministry of Defense plans to cut $10 billion (or roughly €7.8 billion) from its defense budget by 2013. If these cuts are implemented as planned, the entire German Armed Forces will number 180,000 personnel; by contrast, 20 years ago Germany had twice that many active duty soldiers in the army alone, not including the Luftwaffe (German Air Force) and the navy. Germany will have a modest number of well-equipped deployable forces.

The German Army will experience the most significant restructuring of the armed forces, as the other services will mainly endure cuts in personnel and equipment. The new army structure will entail two modified divisional headquarters, six brigades, and a new Rapid Forces Command.[3] This new command will be comprised of one paratrooper and one light infantry regiment, plus one Tiger combat helicopter and two NH90 transport helicopter regiments

Italy

In the face of powerful budget pressures, Italy is attempting to maintain a full spectrum of military capability similar to that of the United Kingdom. Major procurement programs will be sustained, but stretched out.

Like other key NATO Europe governments, the Italian government has underestimated the cost of converting from a conscription system to an all-volunteer force. Under budget pressure, the Italian Armed Forces have had to slash its operations and maintenance budget to ensure the readiness of those forces of brigade size that deploy to the International Security Assistance Force (ISAF) in Afghanistan. As in the case of the French and German armies, the Italian Army will maintain several heavy brigades but at reduced readiness. The ongoing euro financial and debt crises may compel Italy to make further spending cuts that could reduce its ability to maintain the operational readiness of its forces.

Spain

The Spanish Armed Forces are attempting to respond to downward budget pressure similar to that of Italy. All three Spanish services will preserve their major procurement programs by stretching out their 15-year plan to 20 years. This will produce rising unit costs but is regarded in Madrid as the only plausible way to maintain a "full-spectrum force." Similar to Italy, the Spanish Armed Forces have had to cut their overall operations and maintenance budgets in an attempt to protect procurement programs and force structure, albeit downsized. As with Italy,

---

3 "Army—Germany," *Jane's World Armies*, July 22, 2011.

this attempt to sustain a viable procurement account and force structure is hostage to the ongoing euro crisis, the outcome of which may impose draconian limits on future Spanish defense spending.

The Netherlands

The Dutch government has imposed cuts on the Dutch Armed Forces that constrain their capacity to conduct expeditionary operations. All three services have been downsized to the equivalent of a brigade-sized structure. Overall, the Dutch Armed Forces are being reduced to the point where they will have only a marginal capacity to project military power. Their traditional contribution of maritime forces, which are well suited to operating in littoral waters and in high demand in the Alliance, are targeted for reduction as well.

Poland

Since joining NATO in 1999, Poland has become a vital member of the Alliance with significant troop contributions and leading roles in Iraq, Afghanistan, and other international missions (though not Libya). The Polish Armed Forces have recently undergone significant restructuring: In 2008, Poland decided to professionalize its army and ended conscription; troop levels have dropped from 180,000 in 1999 to 100,000 at the end of 2011. In 2009, Warsaw adopted an ambitious ten-year modernization plan to replace equipment, and increase interoperability, deployability, and sustainability.

Poland's defense budget grew by over 50 percent between 2005 and 2010. The budget crisis of 2009 only put a temporary damper on Poland's defense spending and budget growth. It stands out as the only country that has managed to increase its budget—by 7 percent in 2011, with a similar rise expected for 2012. While Poland has the smallest defense budget of the countries examined in this study, it consistently spends close to the 2 percent level desired by NATO. If Poland is able to sustain the same trajectory, its significance as a key NATO ally will also increase.

Impact of Defense Cuts on NATO's Capacity to Conduct Important Military Missions

When viewing NATO Europe's overall military capability in the coming decade, the lack of "quantity" has a qualitative effect. Given the anticipated cuts and future financial constraints, the capacity of the major European powers to project military power will be highly constrained:

- The units of account for European ground forces will be battalion battle groups and brigade combat teams and not full-strength divisions and corps.
- If UK and French forces were to become tied up in a protracted deployment along either the coast of Africa during a counter-piracy mission or while conducting a protracted peacekeeping operation in that continent's sub-Saharan region, they would be strained to execute a time-urgent major Mediterranean expeditionary operation outside NATO. Conversely, if NATO Europe got involved in a major operation in the Mediterranean, it would not likely have the reserve capacity to address long-distant lower-risk contingencies, much less a higher-risk contingency in the Persian Gulf region. At best, the United States can hope that NATO Europe, including France, the UK, Italy, and Spain, can maintain a militarily credible Mediterranean capacity, with the understanding of the limits of that capability.
- In light of the collective NATO experience during its protracted large-scale counterinsurgency operation in Afghanistan, NATO Europe will have neither the will nor the capability to maintain a multi-brigade expeditionary force over a long distance from Europe for a multiyear peace-enforcement mission.

Meeting NATO's Defense Challenges in an Era of Austerity

In light of the cuts currently under way and those that are anticipated, Alliance members will have to find ways to provide security with fewer resources. These include the following:

Pooling and Sharing. As European governments have been forced to make deeper cuts in defense spending, they have begun to pay greater attention to possibilities for pooling and sharing resources. Bilateral partnerships, such as the British-French Defense Co-operation Treaty, may provide a more effective way of reducing costs and producing synergies and should be encouraged. But, while pooling and sharing can help to rationalize defense efforts and reduce costs, they cannot easily make up for sustained drops in defense spending.

Leapfrogging. The strategy of "leapfrogging"—cutting defense expenditures heavily today while investing in new types of capabilities—may also prove to be a more effective way of coping with changing technological realities, emerging new threats, and declining defense budgets than maintaining the old capabilities. Britain and the Netherlands appear to have chosen this path.

Informal Ad Hoc Coalitions. As the Libyan intervention underscored, in the future, internal differences within the Alliance may make it difficult to obtain a consensus for NATO to engage in some missions beyond Europe's borders. As a result, we may see coalitions of allies operating both inside and outside a NATO context. This highlights the importance of sustaining interoperability among U.S. forces and the forces of individual NATO allies. This, in turn, requires maintaining a U.S. force posture in Europe that can be augmented in time of crisis.

Crisis Management in the Maghreb. As the United States increasingly focuses on Asia, Washington should encourage NATO Europe to take lead responsibility for managing future crises in the Maghreb[4]—a region in which Europe, especially the southern Alliance members, have strong historical interests. In this region, the United

---

[4] The Maghreb refers to the area west of Egypt and includes Morocco, Tunisia, Algeria, Libya, and Mauritania.

States would play a supporting role, providing key enablers to European allies who would have the lead in day-to-day combat missions.

As part of this new division of labor, the United States should encourage France, the UK, and Italy, together with Spain, to assume primary responsibility for ensuring peace and stability in the Maghreb and to maintain forces capable of carrying out this task. In particular, the United States should encourage the French and British to widen the scope of their military cooperation to include closer integration of their military forces with Italy and Spain.

British-French Defense Cooperation. The United States should encourage Britain and France to intensify the defense cooperation that they initiated with the signing of the November 2010 defense treaty. This collaboration should help Britain and France to sustain a high-performance naval strike capability to support U.S. efforts to contain Iran's geostrategic influence if Tehran acquires an operational nuclear arsenal. This cooperation is all the more important because of the growth of Euro-skepticism within the Conservative Party and the strong economic constraints on defense spending that the Cameron government will face in the next several years. Britain's firm engagement in Europe is critical to maintaining NATO's political and military vitality in the coming decade and should be strongly encouraged by Washington. Without strong British participation, it will be difficult to build a credible European defense capability within NATO and the EU.

The Weimar Triangle and Baltic Region. Germany should be encouraged to take on greater responsibility for ensuring security and stability in Eastern Europe. The United States should urge Germany to maintain a robust ground force for this purpose. At the same time, Berlin should be encouraged to intensify defense cooperation with Poland within the framework of the Weimar Triangle and to work closely with Denmark and Sweden to ensure the security of the Baltic region. In addition, defense cooperation between NATO and Sweden and Finland should be strengthened.

Acknowledgments

The authors would like to thank the following individuals for sharing their knowledge and expertise with the authors:

Major Reed Anderson, James Appathurai, Robert Bell, Frank Boland, Yves Boyer, Heiner Braus, Gen. Vincenzo Camporini, Capt. Alexander Casimes, Hon. Guiseppe Cossiga, Col Jos Coumans, Hon. Guido Crosetto, Gen. Claudio Debertolis, Lt Col Emmanuel Delorme, Térèse Delpech, Gen. Salvatore Farina, Bastian Giegerich, Anne-Marie Le Gloannec, Niklas Granholm, Andrea Grazioso, Phillipe Gros, Hans-Christian Hagman, Pierre Hassner, Francois Heisbourg, Wolfgang Ischinger, Karl-Heinz Kamp, Chris Keay, Adrian Kendry, Eckhart von Klaeden, John Kornblum, Lt Col Tara Llewellan, Gerard Malet, Commander Duncan McCue, Holger Mey, Michel Miraillet, Gen Klaus Naumann, Manfred von Nordheim, Jean-Jacques Patry, Bernhard Rabert, Jean-Loup Samman, Eberhard Sandschneider, Lt Col Marc Sleven, Stefano Stefanini, Constanze Steltzemueller, Amb. Francesca Tardioli, Col Ralph Thiele, Marcel de Vink, Ian Wallace, Graham Webber, Lt Col Robert Wildenberg, and Mike Winnerstig.

Special thanks go to Kurt Volker and Christopher Chivvis for their helpful comments and suggestions on improving the original draft of the report.

Abbreviations

A&D	aerospace and defense
A2/AD	anti-access/area denial
AFV	armored fighting vehicle
AGS	Alliance Ground Surveillance
ASMP-A	Air-Sol Moyenne Portee
AWACS	Airborne Warning and Control System
C4ISR	command, control, communications, computers, intelligence, surveillance, and reconnaissance
CAS	close air support
CATOBAR	catapult-assisted takeoff but arrested recovery
COIN	counterinsurgency
CROs	Completion Reserve Officers
CSAR	combat search-and-rescue
CSR	Comprehensive Spending Review
CTOL	conventional takeoff and landing
DoD	Department of Defense
EATF	European Air Transport Fleet
EAW	Expeditionary Air Wing
EI	*Esercito Italiano* (Italian Army)
EU	European Union

FREMM	Fregata Europea Multi-Missione
FRES	Future Rapid Effects System
GDP	gross domestic product
HMS	Her Majesty's Ship
HNLMS	His Netherland Majesty's Ship
HTK	hit-to-kill
IED	improvised explosive device
ISAF	International Security Assistance Force
ISR	intelligence, surveillance, and reconnaissance
MALE	medium-altitude long-endurance
MANPADS	man-portable air defense systems
MBT	Main Battle Tank
MEADS	Medium Extended Air Defense System
MoD	Ministry of Defense
NATO	North Atlantic Treaty Organization
NCO	noncommissioned officer
ODIN	Observe, Detect, Identify, and Neutralize
PGMs	precision-guided munitions
PLN	Polish zloty
RAF	Royal Air Force
RNLAF	Royal Netherlands Air Force
RNLN	Royal Netherlands Navy
SAR	search-and-rescue
SAS	Special Air Service
SDSR	Strategic Defense and Security Review
SEAD	suppression of enemy air defenses

SIGINT	signals intelligence
SOF	special operations forces
SROs	Selected Reserve Officers
SSBN	ballistic missile submarine
SSN	attack submarine
STOVL	short takeoff and vertical landing
UAV	unmanned aerial vehicle
UCAS	unmanned combat air system
USAF	U.S. Air Force
USAFE	U.S. Air Forces in Europe

CHAPTER ONE

Introduction

In the coming decade, NATO will have to operate in an environment of growing fiscal austerity and declining defense budgets. The onset of the global economic crisis has forced most European governments to trim their defense budgets: Germany will reduce defense spending by a quarter over the next four years, Britain's defense budget will be slashed by over 8 percent in real terms by 2015, and the defense budgets of some of the smaller European nations have taken even larger cuts. The United States is also planning significant reductions.

These cuts have been driven largely by domestic factors—particularly the need to reduce large budget deficits—not by a change in the nature of external threats. Moreover, the cuts have been made with little coordination with reductions by other Alliance members. If this uncoordinated process of budget cuts and reductions intensifies, there is a danger that NATO will lose critical capabilities and that U.S. and European forces will no longer be able to operate together to meet the growing security challenges confronting the Alliance as it enters the second decade of the 21st century.

The Defense Spending Gap

The cuts come after several decades of decline in defense spending by the European members of NATO. As European countries have become more affluent, they have spent less on defense. Since the end of the Cold War, defense spending by the European members of NATO has declined by 20 percent. During the same period, the combined gross domestic product (GDP) of the European members of the Alliance has grown by 55 percent.[1]

This decline is in marked contrast to trends in emerging powers. Between 2000 and 2009, India's defense spending grew by 59 percent, while China's defense spending tripled, albeit from a much lower basis.[2] During the same period, defense spending in Russia also significantly increased (see Figure 1.1).

The contrast with the United States defense spending during the same period is also striking. During the Cold War, defense expenditures in NATO Europe represented almost 34 percent, with Canada and the United States covering the remaining 66 percent. Since then, the share of NATO's security burden borne by the European members of the Alliance has dropped to 21 percent.[3]

Figure 1.1
Defense Spending of NATO, China, India, and Russia as Percentage of GDP, 2001–2009

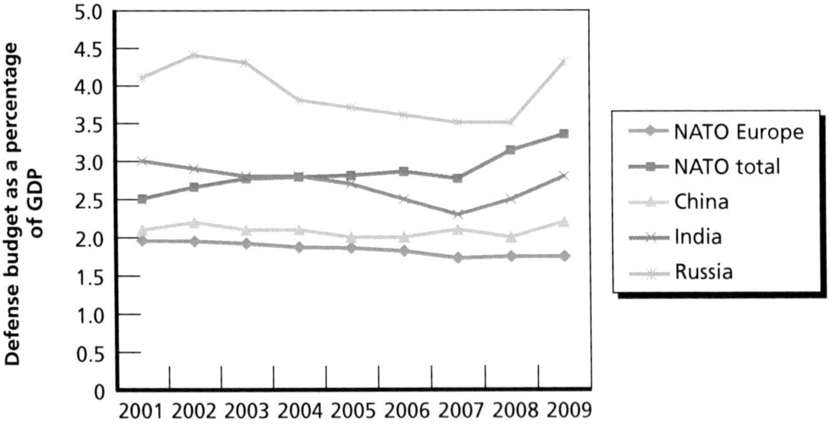

SOURCE: "NATO Semestrial Statistical Memorandum," 2011.
RAND *MG1196-1.1*

---

1 Anders Fogh Rasmussen, "NATO After Libya," *Foreign Affairs*, Vol. 90, No. 4, July/August 2011, p. 3.

2 Rasmussen, 2011, p. 3.

3 Rasmussen, 2011, p. 3.

These trends are even more worrisome because the environment for defense spending is likely to worsen in the coming decade. If the EU fails to manage the sovereign debt crisis more decisively, the Eurozone could collapse, exacerbating the global economic recession and creating further pressures for defense cuts.

Purpose and Organization of the Study

This study assesses the impact of the current and planned austerity measures and reforms on NATO's ability to meet the security challenges of the 21st century. It focuses on seven Alliance members: the United Kingdom, France, Germany, Italy, Spain, the Netherlands, and Poland. Together, these seven countries have the highest proportion of deployable forces in the Alliance. They also have some of the most advanced weaponry and technological capabilities in the Alliance.

The study is divided into five chapters. Chapter Two examines the impact of the current and planned cuts on the armed forces of the seven countries mentioned above. Where do the cuts fall? What impact will they have on NATO capabilities?

Chapter Three focuses on the impact of the cuts on the ability of these countries to contribute to five different missions: (1) defense of NATO territory; (2) missions in NATO's immediate neighborhood (e.g., the Mediterranean littoral); (3) high-intensity power-projection missions in distant regions (e.g., the Persian Gulf); (4) long-range operations with small "conventional forces" (e.g., peacekeeping in Africa); and (5) long-range special operations forces (SOF) (counterterrorism and counterinsurgency [COIN]) operations.

Chapter Four focuses on the strategic context, particularly the impact of developments within the EU and the implications of the 2011 Libyan intervention. How are these factors likely to affect the challenges the Alliance faces in the coming decade? What are the lessons for NATO of the Libyan intervention?

The final chapter examines the implications of the cuts for U.S. policy and U.S. national interests. How should the United States respond to these new challenges? What options does it have? How will the strategic environment help or hinder the choices that U.S. policymakers face?

CHAPTER TWO

The Impact of Defense Cuts on Key NATO Allies

This chapter assesses the impact of recent and anticipated defense budget cuts on seven Alliance members: the United Kingdom, France, Germany, Italy, Spain, the Netherlands, and Poland. These seven countries were selected due to their overall level of military capability within the NATO alliance. Some of them, in particular the United Kingdom and France, have a long record of projecting military power well beyond Europe in addition to being key participants in Article V missions to defend European territory. In the case of Germany, the country has only made limited deployments outside Europe since the Bundeswehr (German Federal Defense Force) was formed in 1955, but Germany was always a key nation when it came to the defense of NATO territory during the Cold War; its army and air force were the largest in NATO Europe for decades. Other countries, such as the Netherlands, have been important because of the capabilities that they provided to the Alliance.

Today very important defense resource reductions are under way that will significantly change all of the seven militaries examined in this chapter. In all cases, the size of the armies, navies, and air forces are being reduced. Importantly, these are not simply "salami slice" reductions whereby a certain percentage of existing force structure or planned equipment purchases are being cut. In contrast to the post–Cold War defense reductions that took place in the NATO European militaries in the 1990s, today several nations are eliminating important capabilities entirely. Additionally, the size of the force structure and manpower reductions are now reaching the point that the remaining air, land, and naval elements are so small that they would experience significant difficulty if a future mission required either a large initial commitment of force or a large rotation base of units and personnel to sustain a protracted operation, such as Iraq or Afghanistan.

In some cases, important capabilities are being entirely eliminated or drastically reduced. Examples include the Dutch decision to eliminate its P-3 *Orion* maritime surveillance aircraft and the decision of a number of countries to cut back significantly on their maritime littoral capabilities, such as mine countermeasures ships. Importantly, since the end of the Cold War the United States has urged NATO Europe to improve its ability to project and sustain military forces beyond Europe, since it is from there that the main threats to European interests will come. Instead, the defense reductions that are about to be implemented in Europe will reduce NATO Europe's capability to project and sustain military power.

This is not to say that NATO Europe is losing all of its military capability. The armed forces of the countries reviewed in this chapter will still retain well-trained personnel and high-quality equipment that are among the best in the world. However, the upcoming defense reductions will, without question, lead to less-capable NATO European militaries.

The United Kingdom

The British Armed Forces are undergoing a period of rapid change. A severe spending cut of more than 8 percent over four years has reduced manpower levels, curtailed equipment procurement, and created capability gaps with the elimination of whole platforms. This has direct consequences for the UK's abilities to carry out current and future missions.

The Royal Navy in particular will undergo significant changes. The decommissioning of the Royal Navy's flagship, HMS *Ark Royal*, has created a carrier capability gap that will last ten years, until the replacement carriers are in service; this has already created difficulties for the Royal Navy's participation in operations in Libya in 2011. The elimination of the Nimrod MRA.4 maritime patrol aircraft program reduces the Royal Navy's maritime patrol and surveillance capability and will make it much more difficult for the Royal Navy to conduct antisubmarine operations in the North Atlantic in defense of NATO territory.

The cuts have also had an impact on the Royal Air Force (RAF) and British Army. The loss of 40 percent of the army's Challenger 2 Main Battle Tanks (MBTs) and of one deployable combat brigade are part of the British Army's reorientation toward a modest-size force that will be far less capable of sustaining high-intensity combat. Within a few years, a brigade-size unit will be the most that the UK can deploy at any given time, and it will have far fewer armored vehicles and artillery to bring to the battle. This means that the British Army will not be able to compete against a North African or Middle Eastern adversary equipped with many hundreds or thousands of fighting vehicles.

In sum, these defense cuts will result in a different British military than the United States has grown accustomed to working with, particularly the British Army. The force structure cuts and structural changes in all components of the British military mean that smaller forces will be available for any given mission, whether the defense of NATO territory under Article V or a future power-projection operation. While the British military as a whole will still be a full-spectrum force, it will be challenged in its ability to conduct full-spectrum operations.

In operations in the Middle East in 1991 and 2003, the British were able to field and sustain division-sized mechanized units with multiple fighter-bomber squadrons for support. This type of engagement is now impossible. In the most recent round of cuts, the British Army has been reduced to an almost pre-Victorian level in terms of active duty numbers. Reductions in equipment and elimination of various platforms make it unlikely that Britain will be able to field a force comparable to that seen in 1991 or 2003 in the foreseeable future. A review of key changes in military spending, manpower levels, force structure cuts, and modernization plans explains why.

Changes in Military Spending

The UK Armed Forces have been forced to make a series of cuts to equipment and procurement that have collectively weakened Britain's ability to participate in major coalition operations outside Europe (such as the Iraq War) or mount unilateral ones like the Falklands War.

In October of 2010, the Comprehensive Spending Review (CSR), part of the Strategic Defense and Security Review (SDSR), instructed the Ministry of Defence (MoD) to cut £8 billion from its 2014–2015 budget. This represents a spending reduction in real terms of more than 8 percent over the next four years.[1] In May 2011, Secretary of State for Defence Liam Fox announced a review of further defense spending cuts after it became clear that the CSR would not ensure sufficient levels of savings.

Changes in Military Manpower Levels

Including civil servants, the total amount of personnel to be cut by the SDSR comes to about 42,000.[2] CSR cuts will cause the army to lose 7,000 personnel, reducing the force to approximately 95,000 soldiers by 2015. The former head of the army, Lord Richard Dannatt, has voiced his concern over the size of this cut, stating that "An army as small as 80,000 will find itself very hard to operate."[3]

The RAF will lose about 2,700 positions in the next few years. In March 2011, all RAF staff were told that approximately 1,000 positions would be cut by September 2011. The first few cuts will comprise 170 trainee pilots, 200 weapon operators, 500 ground staff, and 121 other officers up to the rank of commodore. Finally, the Royal Navy is scheduled to lose some 4,000 navy personnel.

Several air bases have closed, including RAF Kinloss, Coltishall, and Lyneham. RAF Cottesmore and Wittering both ended flying operations in December 2010. Owing to the Tornado GR.4 cuts discussed below, either RAF Lossiemouth or Marham will close. Simi-

---

1 "UK Defense Ministry Looks to Further Cuts," *Jane's Intelligence Weekly*, January 20, 2011.

2 "UK Defense Ministry Looks to Further Cuts," 2011.

3 "Lord Dannatt's Warning About Army Cuts," *British Forces News*, May 11, 2011.

larly, RAF Leuchars will most likely close following the drawdown of the Typhoon aircraft, also discussed below.

Force Structure Cuts

Air Force. The Three Month Review recommended cutting the air force's fleet of Eurofighter Typhoons and Panavia Tornado GR.4s from 210 to below 100. Once operations end in Afghanistan, the MoD plans to retire the Sentinel R. Mk 1, the Hawk 1, and the Nimrod MRA. Mk2. The CSR cuts included the entire fleet of Harrier GR.9 combat aircraft. The Harrier cut has joint implications because the RAF Harriers are the only fighter aircraft available for use aboard Royal Navy aircraft carriers until the international Joint Strike Fighter becomes available in the next decade.

These cuts have stirred considerable debate and controversy. In a letter to Prime Minster David Cameron in January 2011, a group of distinguished British military experts and retired commanders argued that withdrawing the Harrier would eliminate the only fighter/fighter ground attack aircraft the UK has that is capable of operating from roads, damaged runways, and rough airstrips close to where they are needed; of operating from carriers, with their advantage of flexibility of maneuver, avoidance of diplomatic and over-flight problems, and independence from vulnerable land and air supply lines; and of providing air support for expeditionary/amphibious operations at short notice throughout the world.[4]

Britain has a significant intelligence, surveillance, and reconnaissance (ISR) capability gap on the horizon, caused by the cut of one platform without overlap of its replacement. The Boeing RC-135 "Rivet Joint" signals intelligence (SIGINT) aircraft will replace the two remaining Nimrod R.1 platforms; however, the Rivet Joint will not enter service until 2014. To cover the gap, the MoD hopes to partner with the United States via a UK-U.S. task force at Offutt Air Force Base in Nebraska, where RAF personnel would serve with the U.S. Air Force's (USAF's) RC-135 wing until the RAF's Rivet Joints are ready.

---

[4] "Military Experts' Warning over Defense Spending Review," *The Telegraph*, January 29, 2011.

Army. In addition to the loss of 7,000 personnel, the CSR calls for a reduction of 100 tanks and heavy artillery pieces. In July 2012, the British Army announced its new structure, consisting of active duty "Reaction Forces" and a restructure reserve "Adaptable Forces," each with a division headquarters. The former will contain three armored infantry brigades, with only one at a high level of readiness, and the 16th Air Assault Brigade, also at a high level of readiness, for a total of 82,000 troops. Additionally, the Royal Marine 3rd Commando Brigade will be retained with an additional high-readiness capability. The reserve Adaptable Force will consist of a pool of seven "light" brigades that can draw on a mix of light cavalry and light infantry brigades at varying degrees of readiness, with a total of 30,000 troops. Both the Reaction Forces and the Adaptable Forces will be provided combat support (artillery and engineers) and combat service support (logistics) by a ready logistic support brigade drawing on a modest inventory of relevant supporting brigades. Overall, this very austere support structure will allow the British Army to field one armored infantry brigade with one or more battalions for the air assault and commando brigades to provide for a sustainable power projection capability. Homeland security and foreign peacekeeping and stabilization missions will be provided by the reserve Adaptable Forces.[5]

On July 18, 2011, the MoD announced further manpower cuts as a means of offsetting modest spending increases on equipment programs in the British Army, Royal Navy, and RAF. In total, 11,000 active duty troops will be cut and replaced with reservists at lower costs.[6] UK defense officials confirmed that these cuts will mean the elimination of a number of infantry battalions.[7] This additional cut will reduce the army to its smallest size since the Victorian era. According to Jim Murphy, the Shadow Secretary of State for Defence, this

---

[5] "Army 2020: Presentation to the Army Chain of Command 5 July 2012," Secretary of State A2020 announcement, UK Ministry of Defence, 2012.

[6] Andrew Chuter, "UK to Up Equipment Funds, Cut Active Duty Troops," *Defense News*, July 18, 2011.

[7] "Liam Fox Announces Army Cuts but Promises Extra Funds in the Future," *The Guardian*, July 18, 2011.

cut in the army is bigger than the entire current deployment of all UK forces in Afghanistan.[8] The UK's special operations force, the Special Air Service (SAS), will also see a slight reduction in its numbers, losing one of the two part-time SAS battalions and retiring those operators who are too old for combat duty.

Navy. The CSR cut the Nimrod MRA.4 maritime patrol aircraft program and reduced the number of destroyers and frigates from 23 to 19. The Three Month Review called for further reducing this number from 19 to 12 units.[9] The *Invincible*-class HMS *Ark Royal*, the flagship of the Royal Navy, was retired in November 2010 per SDSR guidelines; the *Invicible* class's limited ability to carry aircraft make them unsuitable for modern missions, and the HMS *Illustrious*, the final operational aircraft carrier in this class, will be decommissioned in 2014.[10] In addition, one of the two new *Queen Elizabeth*–class carriers will be placed in "extended readiness" or sold.

The Royal Navy has retained almost the entirety of its amphibious capability. It is keeping the 3rd Commando Brigade of Royal Marines (which the Three Month Review recommended disbanding) under its control instead of passing it to the army, and it has chosen to protect the helicopter carrier HMS *Ocean*, cutting the aircraft career HMS *Illustrious* instead, having had the option of choosing one or the other. It is losing one of the two landing platform/dock (LPD) ships (likely the HMS *Albion*) and one of four *Bay*-class auxiliary landing ships.[11] These cuts may change once the results of the Three Month Review are published.

---

8 "MoD Sacrifices Manpower to Pay for Equipment," *The Telegraph*, July 19, 2011.

9 "Western Europe—Navy—United Kingdom," *Jane's Sentinel Security Assessment*, June 30, 2011.

10 "Western Europe—Procurement—United Kingdom," *Jane's Sentinel Security Assessment*, July 4, 2011.

11 Iain Ballantyne, "The Great Transition: New Royal Navy Abandons Primacy in Maritime Domain," *Defense IQ*, October 27, 2010.

Changes in Modernization Plans

The British are trying to maximize their remaining procurement funds following the latest round of cuts. The British Army is in the midst of planning a major modernization of its fleet of medium weight armored fighting vehicles (AFVs) through its Future Rapid Effects System (FRES) program. The navy is moving ahead with a major F-35B acquisition—the aircraft that is intended to be the main weapon aboard the new aircraft carriers. Britain's national commitment to maintaining its nuclear deterrent might cause the F-35B program to be scrapped.

Looming over all of Britain's future conventional modernization programs, however, is the potentially huge price tag of building three new ballistic missile submarines (SSBNs) to replace the four *Trident* ballistic missile boats currently operated by the Royal Navy. Despite the multibillion-pound cost of the new submarines, the British government considers the retention of a national strategic nuclear deterrent force a vital national interest. This nuclear deterrent modernization plan is going through another government review to address the high costs and strategic relevance of the program. The force size and design of this deterrent force could be significantly changed if the militarily demanding "Moscow Criterion" is dropped (which is the underlying rationale for the continuous at-sea deterrent [CASD] requirement), or in response to a scheduled referendum on Scottish independence. The leading political proponent of Scottish nationalism, the Scottish National Party, has called for the demobilization of the Royal Navy's facilities that support the peacetime operations of the *Vanguard*-class SSBN fleet. Replicating those assets would dramatically increase the cost of the current SSBN replacment option.[12]

Air Force. With the elimination of the Nimrod, the UK loses its maritime patrol and SIGINT surveillance capability. This is an area, however, in which the MoD has evidently taken a calculated risk. According to MoD staff in discussions with RAND, this was the most difficult decision made over the course of the SDSR, and its impact remains the most difficult to mitigate. RAF leadership is fully cog-

---

[12] Dylan Lee Lehrke, "Deterrent Dilemma—UK Examines Its Nuclear Options," *Jane's Intelligence Review*, July 10, 2012.

nizant that this cut leaves it with a capability gap for the immediate future. The leadership is currently engaged in bilateral negotiations with France to assess ways of filling the gap.

Meanwhile, the RAF is conducting a significant procurement program for unmanned aerial vehicles (UAVs). The RAF currently operates six MQ-9 Reapers, and another five are in the pipeline for delivery. This follows a previous announcement that the MoD intends to increase the total number of UAVs to ten or possibly 13. In July 2003, the RAF committed to an £800-million contract for 20 Hawk Mk 128s, followed by another order for 28 more. Delivery of this platform began in 2009. Following November 2010 talks and a signed accord between both governments' MoDs, BAE Systems and Dassault Aviation signed a memorandum of understanding in March 2011 to provide a medium-altitude long-endurance UAVs for both France and the UK.

Army. The Challenger 2 MBT fleet faces reductions of about 40 percent, according to the 2010 SDSR. This would reduce the number of tanks from 345 to 207. This number may be further reduced.[13] All five tank regiments will remain, but half of each will be assigned other vehicles, with details still to be determined.

Navy. The decommissioning of the carrier battle group HMS *Ark Royal* combined with the retirement of the Harrier GR.9 and the delay in the readiness of the *Queen Elizabeth*–class carrier (including the integration of the new Joint Strike Fighter onto the ships) until 2020 means that the Royal Navy will have a significant carrier capability gap.[14] To mitigate this gap, the British and French signed a treaty in November 2010 that will allow British forces to use the French aircraft carrier *Charles de Gaulle* until 2020.[15] Nevertheless, the loss of this capability might also create a knowledge gap for naval aviation operations with fixed-wing aircraft.

---

13 "Western Europe—Procurement—United Kingdom," 2011.

14 "Western Europe—Navy—United Kingdom," 2011.

15 "Western Europe—Navy—United Kingdom," 2011.

Cuts in Training and Readiness

Air Force. With fewer aircraft to fly and a reduction in the RAF's manpower (by 5,000) to 33,000 by 2015, the RAF plans to reduce the number of pilots in service.

Changes in the Nuclear Force

The SDSR concluded that a smaller number of nuclear warheads can achieve the same level of deterrence and therefore called for a reduction of the number of nuclear warheads on deployed submarines from 48 to 40 per boat, and a reduction in the number of loaded missile tubes from 12 to 8. The number of operationally available warheads will fall to a maximum number of 120. This will, it is expected, save the MoD roughly £3.2 billion over the next ten years. In addition, in March 2009 the former Labour government cut the number of missile tubes in the next-generation *Vanguard*-class SSBN from 16 to 12; further reductions have followed. The delivery of this new class of SSBNs has been delayed until 2028, following the Conservative government's decision to refit the current boats extensively.

Nuclear use doctrine was made more ambiguous in that the UK would only consider using nuclear weapons in extreme circumstances of self-defense, including the defense of NATO allies. Britain remains deliberately ambiguous about precisely when, how, and at what scale it would contemplate their use. Furthermore, the UK will not use or threaten to use nuclear weapons against non–nuclear weapon states that are parties to the Treaty on the Non-Proliferation of Nuclear Weapons (NPT).

Changes and Eliminations of Military Missions

In general, the restructuring of the British Armed Forces has been guided by reduced ambitions for future operations. Planning assumptions laid out in the SDSR envisage that the armed forces in 2020 will be sized and shaped to conduct an enduring stabilization operation at around brigade level (up to 6,500 personnel), while also conducting one non-enduring complex intervention (up to 2,000 personnel) and one non-enduring simple intervention (up to 1,000 personnel); or to conduct three non-enduring operations if the UK were not already engaged in an enduring operation; or, for a limited time, and with sufficient warning, to commit all effort to a one-off intervention up to three brigades, with maritime and air support (around 30,000, two-thirds of the force deployed to Iraq in 2003).[16]

According to staff at the UK MoD, the projected ground force of 2020 will be able to handle three types of interventions: (1) one simple, (2) one complex (calling for roughly 2000 troops), and (3) one enduring stability operation. Alternatively, the force will be able to handle three simultaneous interventions, in a surge-type mission. Both simple and complex operations would be non-enduring and last a maximum of 90 days. Two brigades (one heavy and one light) will be held at high readiness for ongoing or possible short-notice missions. For the enduring deployment of army forces, soldiers will rotate at an operational tempo of 1:4—or six months on and 24 months off. To maintain this schedule, it will take five brigades to keep one forward.[17] It would take 180 days to prepare for a major intervention. The army reduced the total number of personnel on operations at any point in time by 20 percent between 2007 and 2009; it now rests at around 16 percent of the army.

The RAF has pivoted from a Cold War footing of air superiority and conventional ground attack to a force focused more on global deployability. Wrapped up in this shift is the reworking of the Eurofighter Typhoon, which now mostly fulfills a CAS function. Additionally, in June 2007, the UK Air Chiefs reorganized six RAF Network-Enabled Capability Programs: Bowman, Cormorant, Falcon, Skynet 5, Watchkeeper, and ASTOR (Airborne Stand-Off Radar). Finally, to enhance readiness, the RAF has developed nine Expeditionary Air Wings (EAWs). Each EAW is led by an RAF station commander, and the core comprises deployable elements of station structures, with the ultimate goal being the rapid deployment of air assets.

The navy has mothballed the last *Invincible*-class carrier battle group, HMS *Ark Royal*. Naval forces will have a significant capability

---

16 "Western Europe—Armed Forces—United Kingdom," *Jane's Sentinel Security Assessment*, August 24, 2011.

17 With the new British Army structure, this implies the call-up of reserve brigades.

gap in carrier naval aviation until 2020, when the new *Queen Elizabeth* aircraft carrier class is slated to become operational. The aircraft carrier configuration will be designed to use only the F-35B, the short takeoff and vertical landing (STOVL) version of the joint strike fighter family of combat aircraft. In the coming ten years, the Royal Navy aviators will be operating with the French Navy from the aircraft carrier *Charles de Gaulle*. The second planned STOVL carrier, HMS *Prince of Wales*, will be built. However, current British plans assume that only one carrier will actually enter Royal Navy service, while the second ship will either remain in reserve or be sold.[18]

Defense Cooperation with France

The UK MoD intensified defense cooperation with France in an attempt to bridge the emerging capability gaps. In November 2010, France and Britain formally signed a defense cooperation treaty. The treaty envisages:

- Joint training exercises to prepare British and French troops for a new rapid-reaction force. The joint force is designed to be modular based upon mission and will be commanded by either a British or French general officer.
- Pooling maintenance and logistics of the A400M transport aircraft.
- Long-term joint R&D efforts, such as satellite communications, cyber security, new missile systems, and UAVs.
- Construction of two new nuclear weapon research and development facilities. This is designed to provide shared but separate testing space.

Although the Franco-British Defence Treaty appears promising along a number of dimensions, including the joint development of a medium-altitude long-endurance armed unmanned aerial vehicle, these important areas of cooperation will be hostage to the willingness and financial capacity of the UK to affect three major procurement

---

[18] "Aircraft Carriers: NAO Fear over Defence Review Change," *BBC News Online*, July 7, 2011.

programs during the beginning of the next decade. These include the acquisition of a naval-fighter fleet to arm the *Queen Elizabeth*–class fighter-vehicle fleet and investment in a follow-on to the *Vanguard*-class ballistic missile submarine program. If the UK does not buy the F-35B, its resulting total inventory of 132 Typhoons by the end of the decade will mean that Britain's air force will not be much larger than Singapore's.

Future Deployability and Sustainability Challenges

During the Cold War, the British Army of the Rhine and RAF Germany provided a large corps-size force backed up by considerable air support for the defense of Germany. In 1991 and 2003, the British were able to field and sustain division-sized mechanized units with multiple fighter-bomber squadrons for support to the Middle East. The current round of cuts to manpower and equipment has made it impossible for the British Armed Forces to deploy a force of that size in the near future.

As shown in Figure 2.1, the UK's defense budget grew by €7 billion, from €41.50 to €48.51 billion, between 2005 and 2008, a 17 per-

Figure 2.1
UK Military Personnel and Defense Spending as a Percentage of GDP, 2005–2010

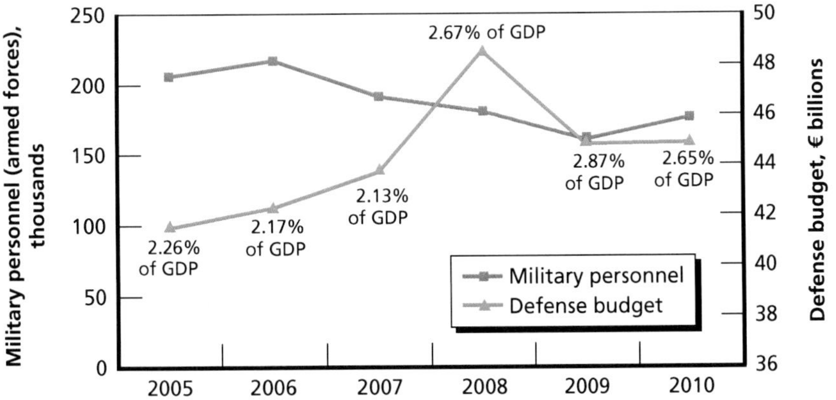

SOURCE: European Parliament, Policy Department, Directorate-General for External Policies, *The Impact of the Financial Crisis on European Defence: Annex*, Brussels, 2011, p. 31.

RAND *MG1196-2.1*

cent increase. However, the financial crisis of 2008 led to a reduction of nearly €4 billion in 2009, and further budget cuts are likely to reduce Britain's defense spending by 7.5 percent over the next four years. Britain, however, has consistently spent a higher percentage of its GDP on defense than the NATO-required 2 percent. Between 2005 and 2010, the UK's defense spending as a percentage of GDP grew from 2.26 to 2.65, peaking with 2.87 in 2009.

Intensifying political pressure for Scottish independence is an important wild card and could affect British defense policy. The Scottish government has said that it wants to be an independent, non-nuclear power and that, after achieving indepenedence, it intends to demobilize the Scottish-based support facilities for British nuclear-powered ballistic missile submarines. While it remains to be seen whether these plans will actually be carried out, and how the costs would be covered, if Britain had to reproduce these facilities on its own territory, this would significantly increase the cost of the *Vanguard* replacement program.

France

Together with the UK, the French are one of the very few European NATO members that have the ability to project and sustain significant military power beyond Europe. The French want to maintain a full-operation military force in the coming years and, unlike in Britain, the French armed forces are not hostage to a looming hefty procurement bill to modernize their nuclear strike submarine force, since that program is nearing completion. However, in the face of significant budget cuts in the years ahead, France will be forced to reduce the amount of military power that it is able to deploy.

The French military has been stretched thin from fighting in three conflicts simultaneously. French peacekeeping troops supported a UN mission to oust the defeated president of the Ivory Coast, Laurent Gbagbo, while French planes attacked government sites in Libya, and French troops served with American forces in Afghanistan.

The global economic recession has increased pressures to reduce discretionary government spending on defense. Among other sectors, the June 2008 French White Paper, which laid out defense planning for the next 15 years, called for a 54,000-man reduction in overall French troop levels, from the overall size of the French force of 320,000, with corresponding budget cuts over six to seven years. The 2011 budget plan also called for an additional 3 percent cut to defense spending through 2013. All told, the strength of the French Armed Forces will be reduced by 17 percent by 2016.[19]

Changes in Military Spending

France's defense budget is currently $51 billion, just under 2 percent of GDP. This is projected to dip below 1 percent as GDP rises, but, in the short term, the defense budget is projected to decrease only marginally until 2014. However, this may prove to be too optimistic—the new Socialist government headed by François Hollande may face pressures to further reduce the MoD budget. At the same time, the 2008 White Paper cut the air force budget by 24 percent, the navy by 11 percent, and the army budget by 17 percent over the next six to seven years.

Following plans to reduce the budget deficit from 7.7 percent of GDP to 4 percent in 2013, former President Nicholas Sarkozy announced his goal of reducing the defense budget by cutting procurement by €3.6 billion.[20] France, however, has a long history of stretching out procurement periods, and delaying these programs will not solve the problem.

Procurement, though curtailed, has not ceased. The navy is expecting to receive a number of new equipment programs. By 2023 the navy expects to have 18 "front-line" frigates (11 FREMM [Fregata Europea Multi-Missione], two *Horizon*, five *Lafayette*), six nuclear attack subs, and the capacity to deploy one or two naval groups, either for amphibious operations or protection of sea lines of communication.

---

19 "NATO Defence Planning Capability Review 2010/11," NATO Defence Policy and Planning Committee (Reinforced), Working Paper AC/281-WP 0049 (R), 2011, pp. 1–3.

20 "Western Europe—Defense Budget Overview—France," *Jane's Sentinel Security Assessment*, March 4, 2011.

France will also have one or two aircraft carriers, four ballistic missile submarines, and four amphibious ships.

The new *Barracuda* nuclear-powered attack submarines (SSNs) are expected to enter service around 2017. Two amphibious force projection and command ships, the *Mistral* and the *Tonnerre*, have replaced the *Ouragan*-class Landing Ship Docks. Each ship is designed to carry 20 helicopters each, more than the current capacity, plus 450 troops and 60 armored vehicles.

Two Eurocopter ECC 225 Super Puma helicopters will fill the long-range search-and-rescue (SAR) capability role of the Super Frelon until the intended replacement, the NHIndustries NH90 NATO Frigate Helicopter (NFH), is ready.

In July 2010, the air force began using an upgraded version of the Air-Sol Moyenne Portee (ASMP-A) missile for use on the Rafale F3 aircraft. The Airbus A400M, a crucial part of France's procurement program, is scheduled for initial delivery in 2013. This aircraft will enhance France's force projection capability.

Changes in Military Manpower Levels

The June 2008 White Paper, which laid out defense planning for the next 15 years, called for a reduction in personnel and aircraft deployed for foreign operations. It recommended that 54,000 personnel be cut from the present 320,000-member force. The White Paper also recommended cutting overseas personnel from 50,000 to 30,000, reducing the number of combat aircraft engaged in overseas operations, and the closure of some permanent French bases in Africa.

Air Force. Of the cuts proposed in the White Paper, the air force would take the biggest hit in terms of manpower. The White Paper recommended that 24 percent of air force personnel be cut, reducing it to 50,000, in addition to reducing the number of combat aircraft in overseas operations. The White Paper recommended that the air force field a fleet of 300 combat aircraft composed of Rafale and Mirage 2000D fighters; however, the latter aircraft's modernization has been delayed.[21] In addition, a number of air bases in France and French air bases abroad have been scheduled for closure (see below).

Army. In 2009, there were 134,000 troops in the French Army, of which 15,700 were career officers and 46,700 were noncommissioned officers (NCOs). Currently, the army has about 130,000 troops. Planned force levels are intended to be enough for three possible contingencies: (1) to support a maximum force of 50,000 troops committed to a NATO-led, high-intensity operation in Europe; (2) to deploy up to 30,000 troops for one year, with 5,000 troops requiring relief every four months; and (3) to support a single 15,000-strong, relievable force indefinitely. The 30,000-troop deployment will be able to deploy "in six months for a year . . . disposing of autonomy with regard to their principle combined operations" and with a capability that will "cover the range" from major, short-term operations to long-term stability operations."[22]

Owing to growing unemployment in France, the army reported that it has three applicants for each available post. Recruiting nets about 15,000 people per year for contracts between three and five years.

Navy. Between 2011 and 2014, the French Navy is scheduled to lose up to 6,000 personnel. However, by all accounts the French MoD will not reduce the number of roles that the navy will perform. In such a climate, France has increased the number of military-to-military partnerships with its allies, especially Britain.

Force Structure Cuts

All programmed force structure cuts are currently part of the White Paper's guidance and as such are not a direct consequence of the financial crisis.

Air Force. The air force is facing three simultaneous changes: conversion to an all-volunteer force, a restructuring of the higher command levels, and a major re-equip program. The White Paper recommended

---

21 "Air Force—France," *Jane's World Air Forces*, July 27, 2011.

22 Jacob Odile, "Défense et Sécurité Nationale: Le Livre Blanc," *La Documentation Francaise*, Paris, June 2008, p. 211.

that 24 percent of air force personnel be cut, down to 50,000 and that the number of combat aircraft in overseas operations be reduced.

At least six air bases in France are to close by 2012. Orange and Toulouse were the first to begin drawdown, followed by Colmar in 2010, Cambrai and Reims in 2011, and Metz in 2012. Five squadrons will disband, and some supporting echelons, including an ELINT squadron with a C-160 Gabriel and a transport squadron with TBM 700s and Fennec helicopters, will be moved elsewhere—current relocation destination is unknown. The C-160 Gabriel will also be retooled to become a SIGINT platform[23]—currently the only SIGINT platform the French have. The closure of Taverny will necessitate that Strategic Air Force headquarters be relocated as well. Those overseas installations scheduled to close are Faa'a (Tahiti), Lamentin (Martinique), and St. Denis (Reunion Island). One of the three *Regions Aeriennes* (the Mediterranean) was disbanded, and the other two (North-East and Atlantic) were reorganized and expanded into North and South. These were subsequently disbanded as well, along with several major commands, most of which were merged into a single Air Forces Command.

Along with the mission change of the C-160 Gabriel, the French Air Force is also retiring the DC-8 Savigne and the DC-8 Rivet Joint. It is also anticipating a shortfall in mobility in the form of a reduction in tankers and strategic lift. Fourteen C-135s will be replaced by Airbuses.[24]

Army. The 2008 White Paper calls for cuts in force levels over the next six to seven years to streamline the command structure and to free funds for new materiel. The White Paper also recommended that the MoD reduce the number of forces it can project abroad from 50,000 to 30,000 personnel, while leaving 10,000 troops on permanent call in France to deal with any threats that arise domestically (terrorism, natural disasters, epidemics, and cyber attacks). By comparison, the 1994 White Paper recommended that the army should have about 125,000 troops ready for force projection, about four times the size. The 17 percent cut in the army budget recommended by the White Paper will,

---

[23] Interview with Phillipe Gros, June 21, 2011.

[24] Interview with French Ministry of Defense officials, June 27, 2011.

some analysts predict, cause France's army to shrink by one brigade over the next five years.[25]

The MoD also decided to close 82 garrisons and airbases, terminate 20 regiments and battalions, and reorganize administrative services. Thirty-three of the units closed are being shifted elsewhere, and most regiments being disbanded are logistic, engineering, signals, or artillery units. None of the 19 infantry regiments will be affected. The MoD also decided to establish 87 interservice "defense bases" to handle the paperwork for military units operating within a 30km radius of the bases.

The number of French Army bases in Africa will be decreased from five to two. One base will be on the Atlantic Coast—Libreville and Dakar are under consideration—and the other will be on the Indian Ocean in Djibouti.[26]

Navy. In April 2010, the French Navy retired the last of its SA 321 Super Frelon maritime helicopters. The last four helicopters operated as SAR platforms, but their high maintenance hours became too expensive. The retirement overlapped with the delivery of the first of two Eurocopter EC 225 Super Puma helicopters. This will take the Super Frelon's place as a SAR platform until the long-term replacement, the NH90 NATO Frigate Helicopter, is ready.

The SSBN force is using only four nuclear *Triomphant*-class submarines instead of six.

Changes in Modernization Plans

Should the French not be able to bridge their budget gap, the MoD has announced that all procurement items will be up for reduction or postponement. However, some sectors, such as nuclear deterrence and ISR, will be examined less thoroughly, to ensure that France retains its critical capabilities. To ensure that these are protected, the MoD is post-

---

[25] Stephen F. Flanagan, Guy Ben-Ari, David J. Berteau, Heather A. Conley, Joachim Hofbauer, T. J. Cipoletti, Roy Levy, and Alessandro Scheffler, "A Diminishing Transatlantic Partnership?" Washington, D.C.: Center for Strategic and International Studies, May 2011, p. 27.

[26] "Army—France," *Jane's World Armies*, July 12, 2011.

poning the modernization of the Mirage 2000D fighter, the Scorpion modernization program for the army, and the Multi-Role Transport Tanker. The planned medium-altitude long-endurance (MALE) UAV order might also be scrutinized. Finally, because the inter-ministerial budget will be used to fund the extra cost of the A400M program, it is unlikely that any new program or equipment buys will be proposed in the next few years.

The MoD is also updating only half of the Leclerc tanks, while cutting the number of tanks to 240. This will cause France to lose half of its armored cavalry.

Elimination of an Important Capability

Trimming the defense budget to close the budget gap, which will include cutting manpower levels, procurement, and force structure will result in some capability gaps. To prevent this from happening, France and Britain have agreed, as noted earlier, to a wide range of collaborative measures, negotiated during a bilateral summit in London on November 2, 2010. Equipment and capability cooperation will be implemented across the army, navy, and air force, including support, logistics, and training for the A400M transport aircraft, joint development of submarines and unmanned aerial systems, and collaboration in maritime countermeasures, satellite communications, and air-to-air refueling.[27]

Burden-sharing with Britain makes strategic sense. Britain and France have a greater level of global ambition and national interests than do other European nations, and both have very well trained and equipped forces backed by robust industrial bases. A partnership will allow both countries to participate in a wide array of missions. By contrast, Franco-German cooperation has been marked by increasing difficulties, as illustrated by the difficulties in deploying the Franco-German brigade in Afghanistan.

---

[27] "Western Europe—Defense Budget Overview—France," 2011.

Cuts in Training and Readiness

The reductions outlined in the White Paper suggest that training for all French military services will be postponed. Meanwhile, the MoD has outsourced the training of French Army pilots to a semi-public consortium called Defense Conseil International.

Planned Changes in French Nuclear Forces

Throughout the Cold War, France maintained an independent strategic and tactical nuclear capability. While the total size of France's nuclear arsenal is smaller today than 20 years ago, France intends to retain an independent nuclear capability. Along with the UK, France will be one of the two non-U.S. members of NATO to have nuclear forces.

The MoD had planned for six nuclear missile *Triomphant*-class submarines, yet only four will be built. However, the *Barracuda* program will construct six new nuclear-powered attack submarines to replace the *Rubis-Amethyste*–class vessels between 2012 and 2022. The first boat will enter service around 2017, the next four will be delivered every two years between 2019 and 2025, and the final vessel will be ready around 2027.[28]

The French Air Force is the only European air component to deploy nuclear weapons. In July 2010, the French Air Force began using an upgraded version of the ASMP-A missile with a range of 250 miles on the Rafale F3 aircraft. This missile will also be fitted to the French naval air wing.[29]

Changes and Elimination of Military Missions

One of the most alarming results of this round of cuts is that only France and the UK will retain significant capability to provide robust forces for littoral combat. This new reality helps to explain the degree to which France has been so open to pooling defense assets with the UK and Germany.

---

[28] "Navy—France," *Jane's World Navies*, August 2, 2011.

[29] "Air Force—France," 2011.

Future operational concepts revolve around new command, control, communications, computers, intelligence, surveillance, and reconnaissance (C4ISR) systems: the Leclerc MBT battlefield management system, the Battlefield Identification Friend-or-Foe (BIFF) program, and the *Système Combattant.*

Future Deployability and Sustainability Challenges

During the Persian Gulf War in 1991, France deployed and sustained a division-sized mechanized force and multiple squadrons of fighter-bombers. Cuts to force structure, size, equipment, and procurement have made that level of engagement impossible for the foreseeable future. This has significant consequences for France's deployability and sustainability, particularly in terms of power-projection missions.

Although France's force structure and modernization cuts will result in a smaller deployable force, France will still be in a select group of European NATO nations that retain a meaningful power-projection capability for operations outside Europe. That is important from the perspective of U.S. military planners, particularly given the fact that France today is much more integrated in NATO planning and operations than at any time since the mid-1960s. The problem is that while France is now much more of an active NATO member, this increased commitment to NATO comes as force structure cuts are reducing the amount of military power that France can deploy outside Europe.

In terms of NATO Article V missions, France will still have the ability to deploy one or two division-sized forces and several fighter squadrons to a crisis along NATO's periphery. The problem will be if France is already engaged in a significant mission outside Europe (e.g., in Africa or the Middle East).

France has partnered with other NATO countries to ensure that it is able to meet its own defense goals. In November 2009, 14 nations of the European Defense Agency signed a letter of intent agreeing to pool their military air transport assets to enhance Europe's airlift capabilities. Belgium, the Czech Republic, Finland, France, Germany, Greece, Italy, Luxembourg, the Netherlands, Poland, Portugal, Slovakia, Spain, and Sweden agreed to form the European Air Transport

Fleet (EATF). Initial operating capacity is scheduled for 2014. Engaged aircraft would include C-130s and A400Ms.

In December 2010, the three members of the Weimar Triangle—Poland, Germany, and France—pledged to strengthen intermilitary coordination and cooperation. A multinational "European Rotary Wing Asset Sharing" project is also in the works. In addition, in March 2011, France signed a memorandum of understanding on future participation in Combined Air Operations Centers and supporting NATO operations. Also involved in the memorandum were Bulgaria, Croatia, Estonia, and Latvia.

France has not yet undertaken any substantial force cuts, with troop numbers decreasing only by 5,500 between 2005 and 2010—from 254,895 to 249,395. However, the June 2008 White Paper envisions substantial force cuts over the course of the coming decade. There was a 16 percent drop in the defense budget from 2007 to 2008: It shrunk from €36.20 to €30.38 billion (Figure 2.2). While France had been able to spend close to 2 percent of its GDP on defense from 2005 to 2007, that average dropped to 1.56 percent in 2008 and did not manage to climb beyond 1.68 percent in 2009. The budget recovered

Figure 2.2
French Military Personnel and Defense Spending as a Percentage of GDP, 2005–2010

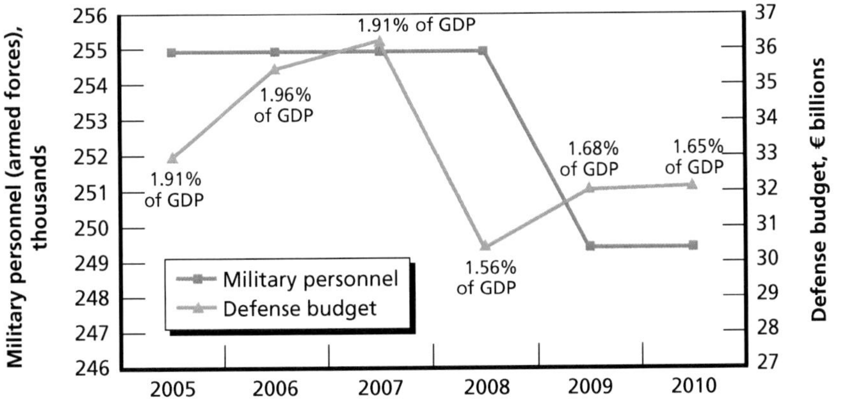

SOURCE: *The Impact of the Financial Crisis on European Defence: Annex*, 2011, p. 11.
RAND *MG1196-2.2*

slightly, increasing to €32.00 billion in 2009 and to €32.10 billion in 2010. No major budget cuts are foreseen in the period to 2014, and the budget is expected to decrease only marginally.

The cuts described above may prove to be the ceiling and not the floor for the reductions in France's military capability, as Minister François Hollande may decide to make further important reductions. The scale and focus of these reductions will be heavily influenced by a strategic review that is expected to be completed by November 2013.

Germany

The German armed forces are undergoing a major restructuring. In 1990, the German army had over 330,000 active duty personnel backed by an additional 700,000 reservists. The current German government is planning on an army of roughly 60,000 men and women. Equipment holdings and modernization plans are both being dramatically cut back to the point that the army of 2015 will number some 12 panzer (tank) *companies* in three battalions. In 1990 the German Army deployed 16 panzer *brigades* in the active force alone, not including reserves. Cuts in the German Air Force, the Luftwaffe, are equally dramatic.

Changes in Military Spending

Defense spending is being significantly reduced. Chancellor Merkel proposed cuts of about €8 billion to the defense sector between 2011 and 2014; with the defense budget in 2010 resting around €31 billion, this amounts to about a 22 percent cut in military spending. This is significantly higher than what other NATO countries have announced. Due to the fact that the MoD was not able to generate this level of savings by 2013—indeed, the reforms meant to consolidate and streamline the force will generate extra costs of about €1 billion—the German Treasury extended the savings horizon to 2015.[30]

---

30 *The Impact of the Financial Crisis on European Defence: Annex*, 2011, p. 16.

Changes in Military Manpower Levels

The total active personnel strength of the armed forces currently is 188,634, reduced from 241,970 following zu Guttenberg's announcement of a 22 percent cut in the armed forces. Force levels are likely to fall further, leveling off at about 185,000.[31] Following the conclusion of the program of cuts, the armed forces are expected to be manned as follows: 37,700 army personnel; 38,800 in the *Streitkraftebasis* (Joint Support Service); 22,700 in the Luftwaffe; 14,500 in the Joint Medical Service; and 13,400 in the navy. These 149,400 service members will be augmented by 34,000 training positions and 1,600 military MoD personnel.

In addition, the Lower House of the German Parliament voted to end conscription and instituted volunteer military training beginning July 1, 2011. The end of conscription was a huge shock. The MoD is concerned about how it will affect the level of missions the Germans can execute. Importantly, every European country that has converted from conscription to a volunteer force has experienced major increases in its military manpower costs, since the armed forces must compete for recruits with the private sector. To some extent, these costs will be offset by force reductions and cuts to other programs.

Force Structure Cuts

Although the Bundeswehr and the MoD have been cut back, the real savings will come from reductions to the current inventory of equipment and future procurement. Active weapon systems to be decommissioned or already decommissioned include six U206A submarines, 15 Transall aircraft, 100 Tornado fighter-bombers, and 60 Marder armored infantry fighting vehicles. Future procurement of strategic and tactical airlift—the A400M transporter and the NH90 and Tiger helicopters—will shrink. The total buy of Eurofighter jets will be reduced, but the final number to be procured remains uncertain. The purchase of more than 100 of the projected 400 Puma armored personnel carriers will be eliminated. In addition, the last transatlantic arma-

---

[31] "Western Europe—Armed Forces—Germany," *Jane's Sentinel Security Assessment*, July 22, 2011.

ment project, the Medium Extended Air Defense System (MEADS) missile defense system, will be canceled.[32]

Army. The German Army will experience the most significant restructuring of the armed forces, as the other services will mainly endure cuts in personnel and equipment. The new army structure will entail two modified divisional headquarters, six brigades, and a new Rapid Forces Command.[33] This new command will be composed of one paratrooper and one light infantry regiment, plus one Tiger combat helicopter and two NH90 transport helicopter regiments.

The number of tank companies will be reduced from 18 to 16, the number of armored infantry companies will be increased from 24 to 27, and the number of light infantry companies is to rise from 37 to 42. All army CH-53 transport helicopters are to be given to the Luftwaffe, while the army will get all NH-90 helicopters that have been programmed to the Luftwaffe. The army will operate one Tiger combat helicopter battalion, with 40 helicopters—down from the original 60.[34] The army is also decommissioning several Leopard II main battle tanks, about 60 Marder infantry fighting vehicles, and a variety of armored anti-air and artillery vehicles.

Navy. Though the German Navy is the smallest of Germany's armed forces, it contributes the highest percentage of its strength to international missions. More than three-quarters of the navy's annual activities take place in cooperation with other nations, primarily NATO and the EU. Therefore, changes to the navy structure are expected to be less drastic than those to the army. That said, the navy can still expect cuts in service and procurement programs. Following the proposed force reductions, the navy is projected to number roughly 13,400 members. In early June 2010, the navy decommissioned its remaining Type 206A submarines in advance of the original 2011–2015 schedule. German officials have acknowledged that reductions

---

[32] Patrick Keller, "Challenges for European Defense Budgets After the Economic Crisis," *AEI*, July 2011, p. 3.

[33] "Army—Germany," *Jane's World Armies*, July 22, 2011.

[34] "Army—Germany," 2011.

in personnel and equipment will make new large-scale missions and lengthy international training maneuvers impractical.[35]

Despite its small size, the navy nevertheless recently launched an ambitious consolidation and reorganization plan. A number of bases have been closed, including Olpenitz (for mine countermeasure vessels), and headquarters merged, leaving four major naval bases: Eckernforde (for submarines), Kiel (mine warfare vessels), Wilhelmshaven (frigates and support vessels), and Warnemuende (patrol boats, which are likely to be replaced by K130 corvettes and/or MKS180 multirole combat ships as the patrol craft are retired in the coming years). By October 2012, Fleet Command and the Naval Staff will be consolidated into a unifying Navy Command at Rostock, and all naval aviation assets will be consolidated at Nordholz and subordinated to a Navy Aviation Command led by a "regimental-level" commander.

Naval aviation has also been reduced to two wings, with the navy's Tornadoes and the naval air station at Jagel transferred to the Luftwaffe beginning in 2005. The two remaining naval air wings—Naval Aviation Wing 3 in Nordholz and Naval Aviation Wing 5 in Kiel-Holtnenau—are now subordinate to Fleet Command.[36]

Air Force. The Luftwaffe, like the navy, will not sustain as significant a downsizing or reorganization as the army. Following modest cuts, the final personnel strength is expected to be 22,700. The air force is also to retire 15 Transall transport aircraft before the A-400M is available. One hundred Tornado fighter-bombers have already been cut ahead of schedule, reducing the total number to 85.[37]

Changes in Modernization Plans

Acquisition cuts might become an important part of the Bundeswehr's savings effort. The German inspector general's report to his cabinet advocated for buying cheaper commercial-grade equipment and cutting acquisition by €9.4 billion. The success of these cuts and of acquir-

---

35 "Navy—Germany," *Jane's World Navies*, July 22, 2011.

36 "Navy—Germany," 2011.

37 European Parliament, Policy Department, Directorate-General for External Policies, *The Impact of the Financial Crisis on European Defence: Annex*, 2011, p. 17.

ing commercial-grade military equipment will depend on the relationship between the MoD and industry.

The navy had originally planned to purchase at least eight new Type 212A submarines; however, funding shortages reduced the second batch of four submarines to two, which will enter service around 2012. The navy will order only three F125 frigates between 2016 and 2019.[38] The role of these frigates has also evolved due to changing priorities and funding issues. The F125 will now be a multirole surface combatant for multinational operations, specifically used for force protection capabilities. As such, it will not directly replace Type 122 frigates.

The navy also reduced its buy of corvettes from 15 to five, with the possibility of an additional five at a later date. The navy's new multirole maritime helicopter buy has decreased from 38 to 30. These helicopters will be deployed on the F124/125-class frigates. Future procurement programs for the Joint Support Ship and two double-hull fuel transporters are also in doubt and may become clearer once the 2012 Bundeswehrplan is announced.

Procurement of the Eurofighter has been cut back to 137, rather than the planned 180. This downgrade might mean the retirement of an entire combat wing—either the JG71 (operating the F-4F at Wittmund) or the JBG33 (operating the Tornado IDS at Buchel). Indeed, all three major re-equipment programs, the Eurofighter, the A400M, and the NH90, have been delayed in some way. Germany will not take the second tranche of Eurofighters but will instead sell them on the export market. Two weapon systems to arm the Eurofighter were also cut. Germany will buy only 1,250 IRIS-T short-range air-to-air missiles instead of 1,812 and will also buy only 480 Meteor beyond-visual-range air-to-air missiles instead of 600.[39]

The number of Airbus Military A400M transport aircraft has been reduced from initial plans to procure 73 aircraft to currently about 47. Final count aside, the new aircraft will play a crucial role

---

[38] "Navy—Germany," 2011.

[39] "Western Europe—Procurement—Germany," *Jane's Sentinel Security Assessment*, July 22, 2011.

in allowing Germany's armed forces to participate in missions for the future European Rapid Reaction Force.

Elimination of an Important Capability

The reduction of the A400M purchase, cuts to German Army strength, and the fact that the German Navy has no amphibious support ships means that the Bundeswehr has a limited ability to project and sustain forces outside Europe. If the acquisition of the Joint Support Ship is also cut, it will represent a further reduction of Germany's already limited ability to project and sustain military forces beyond Europe and its immediate neighborhood abroad.

Cuts in Training and Readiness

No training cuts have been announced, but the government's deep reduction in the number of armed forces, plus the elimination of conscription, will have a profound impact on Germany's overall military readiness. The conversion from conscription to a volunteer military will drive up personnel costs, perhaps dramatically. This could result in further cuts to overall manpower levels, force structure, and procurement.

Future Deployability and Sustainability Challenges

Currently, Germany sends about 7,000 soldiers abroad at any one time. This is a small number compared with the United Kingdom, which can deploy up to 22,000 troops, and France, which can deploy 30,000 troops. After the restructuring is complete, the Bundeswehr is slated to become a more sustainably deployable force, enabling Germany to deploy some 10,000 troops overseas on a continual basis. The key question is whether Germany will be willing to deploy forces in contingencies beyond its borders. The Afghan experience has contributed to a broad public reluctance to deploy German forces in future military operations outside Europe. While Germany may be willing to particpate in Alliance peacekeeping operations, it is likely to remain hesitant about deploying its military forces in multilateral peace enforcement operations outside Europe.

That said, Germany's armed forces have been deeply involved in the International Security Assistance Force (ISAF), with 4,812 personnel deployed in Afghanistan and Uzbekistan as of June 2011. Additionally, as of May 2011, there were 1,130 German military personnel deployed with KFOR, NATO's Kosovo Force, with the Multinational Battle Group South along with Austria, Switzerland, and Turkey. The Bundestag (German national parliament) voted to extend the group's mandate by 12 months in June 2011. German troops also serve in four UN missions: the United Nations Assistance Mission in Afghanistan (UNAMA, one expert), the African Union/United Nations Hybrid operation in Darfur (UNAMID, nine troops), the United Nations Interim Force in Lebanon (UNIFIL, 239 troops), and the United Nations Missions in Sudan (UNMIS, five troops and 16 experts). Twenty German soldiers also serve with EUFOR, the EU's mission in Bosnia and Herzegovina, three soldiers are deployed with the EU's advisory and assistance mission for security reform in the Congo (EUSEC RD Congo), and six are with the European Union Training Mission (EUTM) in Uganda.[40]

Germany's defense budget grew by 32 percent between 2005 and 2010, from €23.5 billion in 2005 to €31.10 billion in 2010, a growth it was able to sustain during the worst parts of the financial crisis. During this period, the percentage of GDP spent on defense increased only marginally, from 1.05 percent to 1.25 percent in 2010 (Figure 2.3). Thus, the 32 percent increase in Germany's defense budget is primarily a reflection of the relative health of Germany's economy and of its need to compete with the private sector for recruits since ending conscription.

Navy. Germany continues to support UNIFIL with a continuous presence of three surface vessels; to support the EU and EU Naval Force's Operation Atalanta antipiracy mission with 1–2 major vessels and P-3C maritime patrol aircraft; contributes maritime combatants to Standing NATO Maritime Groups 1 and 2 and mine countermeasures (MCM) vessels to Standing NATO MCM Groups 1 and 2; and is participating in two major cooperative battlegroup exercises and one cooperative deployment of a German air defense frigate with a U.S.

---

40 "Army—Germany," 2011.

Figure 2.3
German Military Personnel and Defense Spending as a Percentage of GDP, 2005–2010

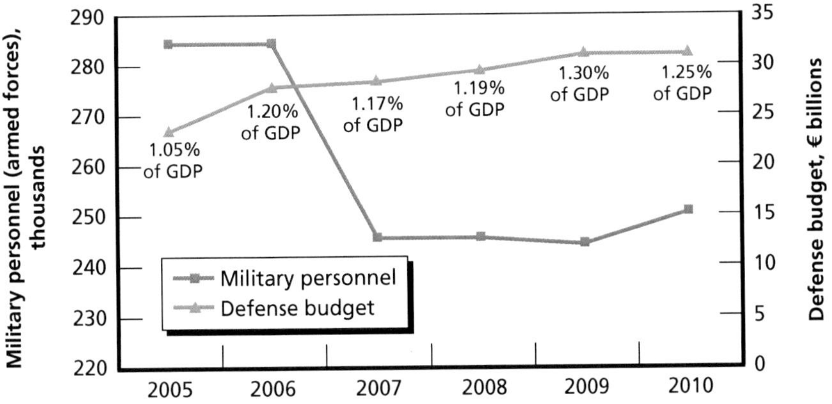

SOURCE: *The Impact of the Financial Crisis on European Defence: Annex*, 2011, p. 15.
RAND *MG1196-2.3*

carrier battle group between 2012 and 2014. This is a significant level of effort.

Four-to-six-month tours and a small rotation interval overstretch the force and can wear on naval vessels. Proposed personnel structure reforms and the designs of new combat ships are both aiming to alleviate these stresses. The navy has begun to rotate crews to maintain a constant presence in theater while minimizing leave time for naval personnel; this is a major change from the "one crew per boat" policy. Ship designs are beginning to take multiple crews into account. For example, the F125 frigate is designed to have a maximum mission duration of up to 24 months, will be capable of sustaining 5,000 sea hours per year, and will have a 68-month gap between major maintenance periods. Its crews should be able to rotate within 48 hours at four-month intervals. In this way, new ship designs are maximizing the length of time that a platform can be deployed, which should have a positive impact on deployability.

Italy

Italy has historically played a major role in Mediterranean regional security. The Italian Navy is the second strongest in the Mediterranean; only the U.S. 6th Fleet is larger. The Italian military is supported by a robust defense industry that produces AFVs, artillery, combat jet aircraft, and major warships up to the size of mid-sized aircraft carriers. In addition to playing a vital role in the Mediterranean, Italy's armed forces frequently participate in operations farther from home. An Italian brigade is currently in Afghanistan, and Italian troops performed important missions in southern Iraq.

Italy's armed forces are experiencing a reduction in funding that makes choices harder and limits their ability to perform the missions at the same level of as in the recent past.

The Italian defense budget is divided into three major areas: (1) investment (what the U.S. calls research and development, plus procurement), (2) personnel, and (3) training, maintenance, and operations. Since going to a volunteer military in 2006, the Italian goal was to spend roughly 50 percent of their budget on personnel, 25 percent on investment, and 25 percent on training, maintenance, and operations. In reality, personnel costs have consumed roughly 70 percent of Italian military spending.

To date, Italy has generally been able to protect its investment account (although there have been some reductions in quantities of ships, aircraft, etc.) as well as personnel. What has suffered, however, is funding for training, maintenance, and operations. In order to maximize the readiness of the units deploying to Afghanistan (and those getting ready to deploy), the readiness of other forces has suffered. For example, the army's heavy armored units have essentially been placed on reserve status, with the tanks parked and the personnel used for other missions. The air force and navy are also starting to suffer from cuts in training and readiness.

Therefore, while the Italians are striving to maintain force structure and manpower levels, as well as press ahead with their modernization plans, a de facto system of selective readiness is taking hold in the Italian Armed Forces. This could, as time progresses, undermine the

Italians' stated goal of continuing to be a full-spectrum force capable of conducting operations inside the Mediterranean region and beyond.[41]

The Italian government has a national debt of 110 percent of its GDP and currently has a budget deficit of more than 5 percent GDP. In July 2010, Finance Minister Termonti outlined a savings program for 2011–2012. This included a 10 percent cut in every ministry's budget—including the MoD. Although the MoD had requested an increased budget for 2011, it is not clear what amount of funding was ultimately budgeted for 2011. The projections for the 2012 military budget are stable at this point, but senior Italian military officials are concerned that additional cuts could come in 2013.[42]

To date, the military's investment (procurement) program has remained largely intact, with some cuts to quantities of systems to be procured. However, the military leadership is concerned that additional cuts in 2013 could lead to important cuts in investment. Italian troops enjoy many of the job security protections of civil servants, which makes sudden reductions in numbers of military personnel very difficult unless there are changes to Italian law governing military personnel.

Changes in Military Spending

The opaqueness of Italy's military spending data prevents a clear understanding of the details of its defense expenditure levels for 2011.[43] According to some open source news reports, Italy was preparing to cut 10 percent of its defense spending in 2011.[44] This follows the defense cuts in 2006 and also in 2009, which were largely due to the fiscal pressures to reduce the public debt. Given the pressure on the overall Italian government budget, additional cuts are likely in 2013 and may continue until the government-wide pressures decrease.

---

[41] Author interviews with senior Italian military officials in Rome, July 25–27, 2011.

[42] Interviews with Italian MoD officials in Rome, July 25–27, 2011.

[43] *The Impact of the Financial Crisis on European Defence: Annex*, 2011, pp. 19–21.

[44] "Recent Defense Spending Plans Announced by EU Member States," *Europolitics*, November 30, 2010.

Operations consumed 12.3 percent of the defense budget in 2010 and are expected to be cut in 2011 to 10.1 percent. As mentioned above, the original Italian goal was to allocate 25 percent of the military budget to operations, training, and maintenance. This funding level is below the minimum threshold needed for operations. As a result, training will likely be cut across all of the forces. Investments in research, development, and procurement have decreased but are still close to the 25 percent goal.[45]

Changes in Military Manpower Levels

Since the mid-1990s, Italy's armed forces have undergone a period of significant change: They have become more professional (Italy ended conscription in 2006) while overall personnel numbers have decreased.[46] In addition, new doctrine and practices have emphasized the importance of joint interoperability, and expeditionary capabilities have increased. These efforts have supported plans for streamlining the Italian Armed Forces, but personnel cuts have mostly affected the *Esercito Italiano* (EI), the Italian Army.

Whether or not these personnel reforms actually enable an enhanced modernization of the Italian Armed Forces is questionable, as cuts in the force structure are often followed by cuts in modernization programs.[47] The two main personnel challenges for the Italian military are (1) the costs of a volunteer force have proved higher than originally estimated (e.g., personnel now account for roughly 60 percent of the MoD budget) and (2) Italian laws make it difficult to rapidly change the size of the force by termination of enlistments or early retirements. The only near-term option the Italians have to reduce total personnel is to curtail recruiting. In discussion with senior Italian military officials, it was clear they understood that the long-term implications of such an approach would result in a steadily aging military.

---

[45] "Western Europe—Armed Forces—Italy," *Jane's Sentinel Security Assessment*, April 14, 2011.

[46] Author interviews in Rome, July 25–27, 2011.

[47] "Western Europe—Armed Forces—Italy," 2011.

Italy plans to decrease personnel costs in an effort to increase the amount of money allocated in the defense budget for investments and training/maintenance. These cuts will likely come from the upper ranks of the armed services and those employed on short-term contracts (between one and four years of service). These personnel cuts will change the demographic make-up of the armed forces—increasing the average age of personnel and shifting the balance of soldiers to officers and NCOs to a ratio of one-third to two-thirds. Because the correct officer mix by age and rank may not be reached until 2021, these trends will impact the operational capability of the Italian Armed Forces, and especially that of the Italian Amy, which relies heavily on enlisted ranks. The armed forces end-strength number was 179,000 troops in 2010. Italy is currently planning to decrease this number to 141,000 by 2012.

Although the defense budget is declining, demand for internal security in Italy remains high. Consequently, the *Carabinieri* budget has continued to increase. (The *Carabinieri* are Italy's militarized national police; they are part of the MoD but also assist the Ministry of Interior combating crime inside Italy.) This is largely due to concerns about illegal immigration and the Italian Mafia.[48] The *Carabinieri* are highly valued by U.S. and NATO commanders in Iraq and Afghanistan due to the high quality of their personnel and their capability to provide a police function in an insurgency environment, including their ability to train local police forces.

Force Structure Cuts

The 2010–2011 defense planning cycle cut one army maneuver brigade (from 11 to 10) and 3–4 navy escort destroyers and frigates (from 16 to 12 or 13). The Italian Air Force will also face cuts. Three combat air bases (Piacenza, Cervia, and Trapani) and a helicopter base (Brindisi) will be closed as part of the Italian defense cuts. In addition, around

---

48 "Western Europe—Defense Budget Overview—Italy," *Jane's Sentinel Security Assessment*, April 14, 2011.

14 airports currently operating on a mixed military-civilian basis will be turned over to civilian authorities.[49]

Changes in Modernization Plans

To fill the capability gap between the retirement of the aging F-104 Starfighter and the fully operational Eurofighter, the AMI has leased air defense aircraft from abroad. These originally included a deal to lease 34 F-16 Fighting Falcons from the USAF until 2010. However, the delay in receiving the Eurofighter has extended this lease. Trapani will operate the F-16 until 2012, and only Cervia will return the F-16s in 2010.[50]

Elimination of an Important Capability

Procurement funds have increased in 2011 in spite of overall defense budget cuts in Italy. Funds for 2011 are €3.4 billion, compared with €3.2 billion in 2010. The budget requests for 2011 include the ability to acquire or support the following:

- a SAR and combat search-and-rescue (CSAR) helicopter initiative
- the development of a laser-based infrared countermeasures system (DIRCM) to protect aircraft from infrared-guided missiles
- rotary-wing programs, including
  - 16 CH-47Fs to replace CH-47 Cs
  - Combat Helicopter upgrades (AW 129 Mangusta)
  - AW 101 CSAR and AW 139 SAR helos
  - NGH 90
  - Textron AAI Shadow tactical unmanned aircraft.[51]

In spite of these increases, the Italian Armed Forces do face the elimination of a few important capabilities. Italy announced in July 2010 that it was reducing its Eurofighter aircraft order from 121 to 96

49 "Western Europe—Air Force—Italy," *Jane's Sentinel Security Assessment*, March 22, 2011.

50 "Western Europe—Air Force—Italy," 2011.

51 *The Impact of the Financial Crisis on European Defence: Annex*, 2011, pp. 19–21.

by cutting the Tranche 3B, a move that will save the Italian government €2 billion.

Several of Italy's naval procurement programs have been cut since 2001. This has included the procurement of two fewer *Horizon*-class destroyers—though the Italian Navy has used the air-defense capabilities of the FREMM to partly fill this capability gap. Unfortunately, the FREMM program is also likely to face cuts. Although plans originally called for ten ships, only six ships are being built. In addition, the last four ships may never enter service. It is unlikely that six FREMM will be able to fulfill all of the necessary capabilities with the current operational tempo.

The Breguet Atlantic maritime aircraft will be retired in 2012 and there are currently no plans to fill its maritime surveillance capabilities. The Italian Navy has also limited *Maestrale*-class frigate upgrades in order to invest in new assets and maintain the *Audace*-class destroyer, *Ardito*, in light of the delays in the *Horizon* Destroyer Program. However, "navy officials are concerned that a prolonged period of reduced efficiency could lead to a more permanent reduction in capabilities."[52]

New acquisition priorities include fighter aircraft, multirole frigates, air-defense frigates, NH90 medium transport helicopters, MEADS, air-to-air missiles, support vehicles, satellite-based communication, and UAVs. The Italians have also expressed desire for the procurement of navy and air force AW 101 helicopters and the procurement of an M-346 Master advanced jet trainer.

Perhaps the most important capability gap that could appear is in the area of missile defense. The recent U.S. decision to eliminate MEADS, which was envisioned as the replacement to the Patriot, will leave Italy without a meaningful land-based missile defense capability. Italy and Germany were both participants in MEADS.

Cuts in Training and Readiness

Cuts in training and readiness will take a big hit in this round of defense cuts. Since 2006, the training fund for the Italian Armed Forces has

---

52 "Western Europe—Navy—Italy," *Jane's Sentinel Security Assessment*, April 14, 2011.

decreased by 69 percent.[53] From 2006 to 2011, the amount of money dedicated to army training funds has decreased from €37.4 million to €11.7 million. Training has been focused only on units due to be deployed.

The School's Command was eliminated and turned over to the Training Command and Army School of Application. The EI had planned to build Combat Training Centers at Capo Teulada, Sardinia, and Monteromano aimed at armored and mechanized forces and to include a combat village as part of its training program. However, cuts in the budget have prevented the establishment of the simulation program. It is unclear whether or not these plans will be continued if funds become available in the future.[54]

Cuts in Italy's defense budget have also impacted the Italian Navy's training budget. Between 2006 and 2011, the navy training budget was cut from €33.3 million to €12.6 million. Engine running hours have been reduced in an attempt to save fuel. This has had a direct impact on the amount of running hours needed for training. Sufficient crew training requires 110,000 hours of motion, but the fleet only sailed around 60,000 hours in 2009.

Changes and Elimination of Military Missions

Italian troops are currently deployed in three theaters: Afghanistan, Lebanon, and Kosovo. The number of brigades does not currently allow for a desired 4:1 ratio of resting brigades to deployed brigades. Further defense cuts will impact Italy's capacity to sustain these missions for long periods of time.

By the end of 2011, the number of Italian troops deployed in foreign theaters of operation will decrease by 2,078 personnel—bringing the total number of troops deployed to less than 8,000.[55] Italy will also

---

53 *The Impact of the Financial Crisis on European Defence: Annex*, 2011, pp. 19–21.

54 "Western Europe—Army—Italy," *Jane's Sentinel Security Assessment*, April 14, 2011.

55 Paolo Valpolini, "Italy Cuts Funding for Libyan Operations," *Jane's Defense Weekly*, July 8, 2011.

withdraw its forces from the Democratic Republic of Congo by the end of 2011.[56]

If Italy has to provide forces for protracted stability missions in the Mediterranean, the reduced size of its army means that the total force that Italy could deploy and sustain would be smaller than today. The *Caribinieri* would probably have to make additional commitments compared with today in order to make up for the smaller EI.

Italy announced that it would cut its expenditures on Libyan operations by more than half on July 7, 2011. The budget would decrease from €142 million in the six months prior to July 2011 to €60 million in the six months after, and Italian support would end at the end of September 2011. Defense Minister La Russa also announced that Italy will cut its personnel in Lebanon from 1,800 to 1,000. No cuts are currently planned for Italian forces deployed to Afghanistan. However, changes may take place in 2012 that could force a revision of this decision.

Given Europe's dependence on Middle Eastern oil, Italy has in the recent past considered the Persian Gulf region an area of strategic importance. Today Italy would be able to deploy a carrier-centric naval task force with several surface combatants, several brigades of army troops, and several fighter squadrons to the region—although such a deployment would take considerable time if limited to Italian military and commercial air and sea lift.

Future Deployability and Sustainability Challenges

Italy is facing substantial challenges in sustaining its force during operations. Operation and maintenance funds decreased by 29 percent from 2008 and 2009 and by 7 percent from 2009 to 2010, with additional planned for 2011.

Modernization and maintenance of equipment was underfunded in 2010 and is likely to remain so—having a direct impact on readiness and sustainability. The goal of the EI is to be able to contribute to three low-intensity operations, two medium-intensity operations and one low-commitment simultaneously. In 2011, the EI engaged in

---

[56] Valpolini, 2011.

one medium mission (Afghanistan) and two low-intensity operations (Kosovo and Lebanon). It is doubtful that Italy can contribute much more. According to the Minister of Defense Ignazio La Russa, it would be difficult for the EI to deploy and sustain 12,000 soldiers today, as it did while operating in Iraq.

The EI also desires to be able to deploy an expeditionary land task force for up to six months in the event of a high-intensity combat operation. However, as of 2011, the EI does not have a large pool of reserves. The EI has two types of reservists: Completion Reserve Officers (CROs) and Selected Reserve Officers (SROs). CROs serve in the army as conscript officers and are slowly being reduced. SROs possess professional skills that are not traditional military skill sets, such as civil engineers, language specialists or layers.

Budget cuts have severely limited army training. Only units getting ready to deploy are given adequate training, leaving the other forces stagnate. The current operational tempo has resulted in large numbers of units in recovery at any given point in time.

In the 2009–2010 cycle, budget cuts to the Italian Navy have decreased supplies of spare parts, fuel and lubricants, and clothing. Intermediate-level asset maintenance programs were also reduced. This trend is likely to continue from 2011 into 2012. "The most recent Navy Annual Report warns that this puts the certain assets at a risk of paralysis."[57]

Italy has not expressed interest in increasing further pooling and sharing options aside from the creation of the Franco-Italian Brigade in spring 2010 and cooperating with the UK on a MALE UAV. Undersecretary of Defense Guido Corsetto expressed concern when the Franco-British cooperation over MALE UAVs did not include Italy.[58]

Italy has withdrawn its participation in the NATO C-17 Strategic Airlift Component, and budget constraints will reduce the Italian Air Force's total force of 390 aircrafts to 310 in the future. Although it is not entirely certain, programs such as the Maritime Multirole Aircraft and the Airborne Early Warning aircraft also appear to be at risk.

57 "Western Europe—Navy—Italy," *Jane's Sentinel Security Assessment*, April 14, 2011.

58 *The Impact of the Financial Crisis on European Defence: Annex*, 2011, pp. 19–21.

The end of conscription in Italy in 2006 resulted only in a marginal cut of force size, with troop numbers dropping from 191,875 in 2005 to 185,235 in 2010. The defense budget experienced a 13 percent cut in 2006, from €14.00 billion down to €12.12 billion, and another cut by 6 percent in 2009, from €16.40 to €15.40 billion, largely due to pressures to reduce the size of Italy's public debt. Despite an overall defense budget growth of 11 percent, from €14.00 billion in 2005 to €15.50 billion, in 2010, Italy continues to underperform when it comes to the percentage of GDP spent on defense, which has ranged from 0.82 percent in 2006 to 1.05 percent in 2008 (Figure 2.4).

Figure 2.4
Italian Military Personnel and Defense Spending as a Percentage of GDP, 2005–2010

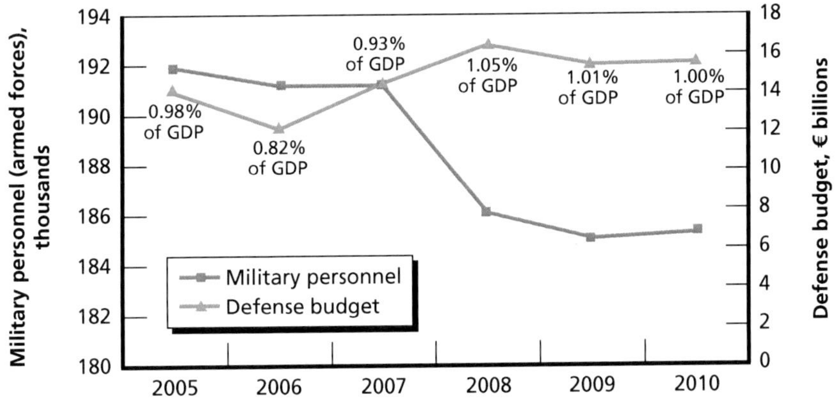

SOURCE: *The Impact of the Financial Crisis on European Defence: Annex*, 2011, p. 19.
RAND *MG1196-2.4*

Spain

The Spanish defense budget rose moderately throughout the first half of the decade. However, when the global economic crisis began rippling across Europe in 2008, Spain took a bigger hit than other Western European states, and its defense budget was cut three separate times. The first cut—a modest 3 percent—came in 2009, followed by a 6.2 percent cut in 2010 and a much larger cut of 13–14 percent in 2012. The budget currently stands at €8 billion instead of the originally planned €9.33 billion.[59] Although the defense budget has been significantly reduced, Spain has not disclosed any plans to reduce commitments, missions, or capabilities or force structure.

Changes in Military Spending

Spain has endured three rounds of spending cuts. The most recent reduction in 2010 cut defense spending by 9 percent, one of the highest cuts sustained in Europe. Most of the cuts in military spending will occur in the procurement category. For instance, €771 million has been planned for procurement in 2011—a major reduction from initial planned procurement of €9.33 billion.[60] Spain has decreased its spending on defense materiel by more than 50 percent since 2008, and since that time the defense sector's share of GDP has decreased from 0.77 percent to a little over 0.6 percent.[61] Although the economic situation continues to decline in Spain, it is unclear what further cuts may occur in the next ten years.

Changes in Military Manpower Levels

The third consecutive cut to Spain's defense budget in 2010 included a 7 percent cut in troop strength in 2011 and 2012.[62] The MoD announced in October 2010 that the bulk of these personnel cuts would be borne by administrative personnel, not the armed forces.[63] Nevertheless, the pay of soldiers has already decreased by 5 percent, and around 6,000 jobs in the armed services will be cut. Most impor-

---

[59] "Spain," *The Military Balance*, London: International Institute for Strategic Studies, September 20, 2011.

[60] *The Impact of the Financial Crisis on European Defence: Annex*, 2011, pp. 25–27.

[61] David Ing, "Spanish Defence Spending Down 50 Per Cent Since 2008," *Jane's Defence Weekly*, July 6, 2011.

[62] "Western Europe—Armed Forces—Spain," *Jane's Sentinel Security Assessment*, March 7, 2011.

[63] "Recent Defence Spending Plans Announced by EU Member States," 2010.

tantly, following defense cuts, the total number of military personnel will be close to 83,000. This will mean that about 1,050 will be cut in 2011.[64]

The current end strength of the Spanish Armed Forces is approximately 128,000 troops. The armed forces also currently employ 26,800 civilians, and the Civil Guard employs 73,000 soldiers.[65] It remains unclear how each of the individual services will be affected by cuts to defense budget. The air force, army, and navy will all likely lose personnel or see positions vacated by retired officers.

Force Structure Cuts

The navy has been reorganized such that all naval forces are under a sole command. A number of smaller units have been decommissioned, such as patrol boats in service for 40 years or more; these have been replaced with smaller vessels capable of participating in maritime security.[66]

Changes in Modernization Plans

The funds dedicated to "general modernization" of the armed forces decreased from €319 million to €283 million in 2011. Cuts in these areas are expected to continue. Plans to decrease the fund to €184 million in 2012 and to €162 million have already been made. It is expected that modernization funds may increase to previous levels of investment again in 2014.[67]

The Leopard 2 tank and the EF-2000 fighter jet suffer the most from these planned cuts. Modernization for modern ground attack helicopters (Tiger) will be preserved, as these are an urgent requirement for Spanish troops in Afghanistan. The Spanish remain committed to "enhancing mobility and projection, sustainability, readiness, surviv-

---

64 "Western Europe—Armed Forces—Spain," 2011.

65 *The Impact of the Financial Crisis on European Defence: Annex*, 2011, pp. 25–27.

66 Author interviews with Spanish defense personnel, September 20, 2011.

67 Discussion with Spanish military officials in Washington, D.C., September 20, 2011.

ability, command and control, ISTAR, interoperability and 'jointness' between the services."[68]

Spain's air force has been stretched thin while waiting for the A-400M to become operational. The delay has forced an extension of current units, which has in turn siphoned resources away from other critical projects.[69] In other areas of the air force, modernization plans continue apace. For example, Spain has committed to upgrading 67 F-18 Hornets, 20 F-5s, 12 C-130s, and six CN-235Ms.[70]

Modernization in the army is relatively modest. The Spanish Army received 646 BMR-600 armored personnel carriers and 342 VEC expeditionary cavalry scout vehicles; the majority of these vehicles are being upgraded to a new common automotive standard.[71] Procurement continues tentatively. In September 2011, Spain approved a major order of 76 Iveco Lince light multirole vehicles and 20 BAE Systems Nyala RG-31 mine-protected armored personnel carriers. Once delivered, the vehicles are to be sent to Afghanistan, with a few remaining in Spain for training purposes.[72] Other modernization plans might also be curtailed. Tranche 3B of the Eurofighter order, numbering about 14 planes, may be cut.

The Spanish Navy has no modernization plans, and procurement will be delayed if the military is to stay within its current restrictive budget.

Elimination of an Important Capability

Spain's overall objective is to keep a balanced range of capabilities, with an emphasis on continuing to transition to a more deployable and sustainable force.[73] Although the procurement budget for new helicopters, transport planes, fighters, tanks, frigates, and submarines decreased by 39 percent in 2010, most of the cuts to procurement will take place on

---

68 *The Impact of the Financial Crisis on European Defence: Annex*, 2011, pp. 25–27.

69 Interviews with Spanish defense personnel, Washington, D.C., September 20, 2011.

70 "Air Force—Spain," *Jane's World Air Forces*, August 12, 2011.

71 "Army—Spain," *Jane's World Armies*, March 7, 2011.

72 "Spain Makes New Vehicle Order," *Jane's Defence Weekly*, September 12, 2011.

73 Interviews with Spanish defense personnel, Washington, D.C., September 20, 2011.

future procurement decisions.[74] The army specifically will enhance its expeditionary capability at a slower pace than other services. Spain is increasing the mobility of its heavy units and ensuring that heavy units can provide greater firepower to light units.

In November 2010, the Spanish Minister of Defense, Carme Chacon, noted that some of Spain's main procurement contracts may have to be re-programmed and payments delayed if the military is to remain within budget. However, she also stated that Spain would not cut any of its large military procurement programs, even in light of the planned 7 percent decrease in materiel spending.[75] Specifically, the current approach is to stretch out major procurement programs under way by turning the current 15-year defense procurement plan into a 20-year plan.[76]

Chacon said that budget cuts would not impact key procurement programs, especially the Airbus A400M transport program. It is still possible that the number of Eurofighters procured will decrease. The Tranche 3B is a likely target.[77]

Cuts in Training and Readiness

According to Spanish defense officials, one of the ways the Spanish have ensured continuity of capabilities in the face of spending constraints has been to reduce overall training levels. Spain now prioritizes readiness of units that carry out operations over training other units for other scenarios. All units are no longer required to undergo training to reach an established standard. This has resulted in an overall shortage of units able to participate in demanding operational environments.[78]

Meanwhile, the Spanish Navy is worried about being able to attract and retain specialty staff with the professionalization of the military. Manning problems have hurt the Spanish Navy's ability to

---

74 *The Impact of the Financial Crisis on European Defence: Annex*, 2011, pp. 25–27.

75 "Western Europe—Navy—Spain," *Jane's Sentinel Security Assessment,* May 19, 2011.

76 Interview with Spanish Defense Attache, Washington, D.C., September 20, 2011.

77 "Air Force—Spain," *Jane's World Air Forces,* March 21, 2011.

78 Interviews with Spanish defense officials, Washington, D.C., September 20, 2011.

deploy multiple units at a short notice. The looming budget cuts will likely worsen this problem.[79]

Changes and Elimination of Military Missions

Spain does not foresee any significant changes to its ability to execute military missions. Spanish officials told RAND that Spain will continue to participate in current operations that require international commitments. However, since the financial crisis affected Spain more severely than most other European countries, it is possible that Spain will reorient its armed forces to align with budget constraints.

Future Deployability and Sustainability Challenges

The cost of overseas military missions does not fall under the Spanish defense budget. This makes it difficult to extrapolate how the budget cuts will impact Spanish deployments in multinational efforts that Madrid supports, such as the EU Battle Group concept and closer coordination with NATO and the UN. However, the Spanish have not expressed interest in pooling and sharing and remain an observer in the European Air Transport Command initiative. Spain has stated that it wants to maintain full-spectrum capabilities independently.

Spain decreased its engagement in the Balkans in order to free its capacities, but has otherwise not discussed decreasing its level of ambition for NATO forces.[80]

Spain does not intend to decrease its spending for military operations in Afghanistan. Chacon said in June 2011 that cuts "might increase risks against Spanish soldiers which completely rules out this issue (of budget reduction)."[81] She went on to affirm that because of concerns of Spanish forces in Afghanistan, the government "will not take any decision to reducing the budget of operations in Afghanistan."[82]

---

79 "Western Europe—Navy—Spain,"2011.

80 *The Impact of the Financial Crisis on European Defence: Annex*, 2011, pp. 25–27.

81 "Spain Won't Reduce Budget for Afghanistan's Military Mission—Min. Chacon," *Kuwait News Agency (KUNA)*, June 21, 2011.

82 "Spain Won't Reduce Budget for Afghanistan's Military Mission," 2011.

Spain's defense budget grew by 14 percent from 2005 to 2008, from €7.12 billion to €8.14 billion. However, the economic crisis led to a 7 percent drop between 2008 and 2010, with a reduction of the budget down to €7.6 billion. This drop, combined with Spain's relatively low defense expenditure and a very low percentage of GDP spent on defense—ranging from 0.72 percent to 0.78 percent (Figure 2.5)—makes Spain one of the worst performers in terms of defense expenditure in Europe. Spain's troop numbers shrunk between 2009 and 2010 by 14 percent—from 149,150 down to 128,000. Given that the Spanish economy is unstable and may continue to decline, there may be further budget and personnel cuts in the coming years.

Figure 2.5
Spanish Military Personnel and Defense Spending as a Percentage of GDP, 2005–2010

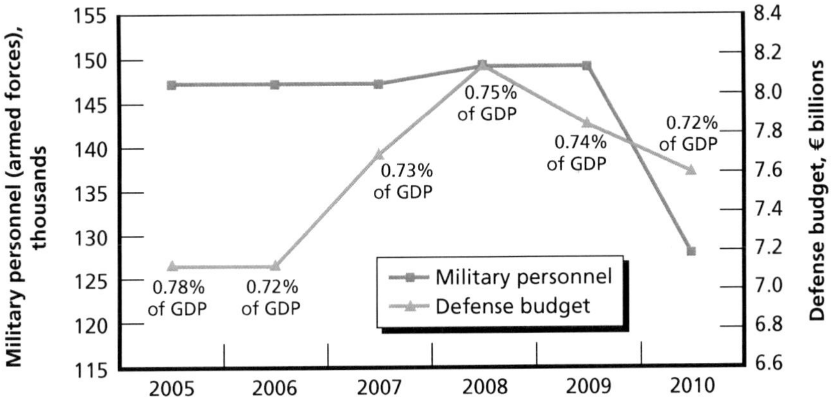

SOURCE: *The Impact of the Financial Crisis on European Defence: Annex*, 2011, p. 25; figure of €7.6 billion for 2010 is from Steven Fidler, "Cutting Defense Around Europe," *WSJ Blogs: Real Time Brussels*, June 25, 2010.

NOTE: The 0.72 percent of GDP figure for 2010 cannot be fully confirmed.

RAND *MG1196-2.5*

The Netherlands

Until recently, the Netherlands maintained ground, maritime, and aviation forces that were generally equipped with near-state-of-the-art weapons. During recent years, the Dutch have participated in operations outside Europe, most notably in Afghanistan, where both ground and air elements (in particular, Apache attack helicopters) were part of the NATO force deployed to assist the government in Kabul. The Dutch have made useful contributions given their country's size.

The upcoming Dutch defense cuts are significant. All elements of the armed forces will see reductions, and a number of important capabilities important to the Alliance will be eliminated. These include the P-3 Orion maritime reconnaissance aircraft and the army's main battle tanks. The Dutch are also reducing their fleet of mine countermeasure ships, traditionally a valuable niche contribution to Alliance forces. Taken together, the Dutch military will, by mid-decade, be less balanced and smaller. It will retain less capacity to project and sustain forces outside Europe and to operate in shallow or confined waters.

The economic downturn has caused budget cuts across the entire Dutch MoD, and defense spending is projected to continue to fall until the economy recovers. In November 2010, the Dutch MoD announced that it would cut 10,000 jobs by 2015 in addition to cutting its overall spending. The Dutch recognize that this will result in the loss of capabilities and also decrease the deployability of their forces. Nonetheless, the MoD has stated that the Dutch Armed Forces will focus on maintaining their essential operational capabilities and acquire more capabilities in the areas of expeditionary operations, network-centric warfare, new weapons, and unmanned and semi-autonomous systems.[83]

The Dutch are expected to continue on this trajectory until 2014. Dutch officials maintain that they expect to balance the financial shortfalls by then and recover from their current economic problems.

---

[83] "Western Europe—Procurement—Netherlands," *Jane's Sentinel Security Assessment*, June 17, 2011.

Changes in Military Spending

The Netherlands has planned a 13 percent reduction in defense spending through 2015.[84] Defense savings priorities have been in the area of management, overhead, and support and operational capabilities. The most recent budget has dictated €200 million in cuts from defense spending. The MoD will have to cut €600 million from its budget over the course of the next four years. These will postpone the delivery of spare parts and affect the maintenance of installations and military equipment.[85]

Changes in Military Manpower Levels

The impending personnel cuts will affect all the services. The armed services will lose 12,300 personnel, while the staff and management will lose 3,300 personnel. About half of these cuts will be through voluntary redundancies. The following is a breakdown of the changes in military personnel by service; with the exception of the Royal Netherlands Navy, all of the sectors of the armed forces will be reduced:

- Navy: 9,800 to 10,100
- Army: 23,700 to 18,600
- Air Force: 8,400 to 7,800
- Military Police: 6,600 to 6,000
- Support: 7,800 to 7,000.

The Dutch MoD has acknowledged the potential consequences of these decreases in personnel. Defense Minister Hans Hillen warned that the armed forces will be less combat-ready and less deployable during the transition phase. Only in 2014 are they projected to be in good shape again.[86]

---

84 Interview by RAND personnel with Dutch military officials at the Dutch Embassy, July 2011.

85 "Western Europe—Armed Forces—Netherlands," *Jane's Sentinel Security Assessment*, June 13, 2011.

86 "Western Europe—Armed Forces—Netherlands," 2011.

Force Structure Cuts

The April 2011 White Paper indicated that both of the Netherlands' tank battalions will be disbanded, and the army's mechanized infantry will be reduced to four battalions from six. In addition to this, two ground installation defense platoons will be cut.

Changes in Modernization Plans

The Royal Netherlands Air Force (RNLAF) is most affected by the recent round of defense cuts in regards to modernization plans. Upgrades to the Patriot air defense systems have been delayed, and Cougar helicopter upgrades will not include engine updates that allow it to operate in hot climates, a key capability in short supply in the Alliance. Although upgrades have been made to the F-16s still in service, budget constraints will constrain future upgrades.[87]

Elimination of an Important Capability

The Netherlands has proposed some severe cuts to its existing capabilities. The number of fast aircraft that the RNLAF possesses will continue to decrease, from 218 to 87. The April 2011 "Defense After the Credit Crisis" White Paper decreased the number of F-16s from 87 to 68. The Netherlands MoD maintains that the RNLAF will continue to be focused on the Joint Strike Fighter Program, even though the government has delayed the procurement of the F-35s.

In addition, the RNLAF stands to lose much of its air transport capabilities. All 17 of the Netherlands' AS 53 U2 Cougar transport helicopters will be cut, although eight will remain until 2017. This will place more importance on the introduction of five new Chinook CH-47F and 20 NH90 helicopters, which will be acquired only when funding is available. The RNLAF will likely rely on its current inventory of 17 Chinook helicopters in the meantime, although upgrades to their engines have been postponed. The single DC-10 transport aircraft will be in service until its planned phase-out in 2013, but no replace-

---

[87] "Western Europe—Air Force—Netherlands," *Jane's Sentinel Security Assessment*, June 17, 2011.

ment has been discussed thus far. However, the air force does plan to maintain its KDC-10 tanker and transport aircrafts as well as four C-130s.

The RNLAF also faces the cancellation of its purchase of six AH-64D attack helicopters, forcing it to rely on its current inventory of 29 Apache helicopters.[88]

The Royal Netherlands Navy (RNLN) stands to lose capabilities as a result of the recent and planned defense cuts. The RNLN faces the cancellation of a new land attack corvette. In addition, many of its frigates will be sold, including two M-frigates and two L-frigates. These sales are occurring amidst the decision to reduce the acquisition of spare parts for the *De Zeven Provincien*–class frigates and to postpone the replacement of the RNLN's unreliable generators.

The combat support ship HNLMS *Zuiderkruis* will be retired in 2011, and the HNLMS *Amsterdam* will be retired in 2014. This will leave a gap in the RNLN's replenishment-at-sea capabilities for at least a year, as the navy is looking to acquire a Joint Support Ship. Reintroduction of RNLN minesweeping ability has also been delayed. In the meantime, the Navy faces the loss of four out of its ten *Alkmaar*-class mine hunters.

The RNLN has planned to retire its fleet of 13 P-3C Orion Maritime Patrol Aircraft. The Dutch have also revised their plans for their four new *Holland*-class patrol vessels. Upon completion of construction, two of the four will be sold immediately. These decisions will likely hinder the Netherland's counter-piracy missions, though the Royal Navy is still planning to acquire four offshore patrol vessels as recommended in the 2005 Naval Study.

The RNLN's intent to sell its equipment is widespread. The navy is looking to sell 21 of its F-16 MLU aircraft, and it has decided not to procure Tomahawk cruise missiles for its frigates.[89]

---

88 "Western Europe—Air Force—Netherlands," 2011; "NL Defense Post-Financial Crisis," *Defensie Afdeling*, August 11, 2011.

89 "Western Europe—Navy—Netherlands," *Jane's Sentinel Security Assessment*, June 13, 2011.

The Royal Netherlands Army also faces sizable cuts to current capabilities. The April 2011 White Paper indicates that all of the army's 60 Leopard 2A6 tanks will be sold, and this intent has been reported to NATO officials. The recently upgraded MBTs will also be sold. As of now, the M1A1 Abrams program will continue.

Six German self-propelled PzH 2000 howitzers, which were brought into service in 2005, are currently scheduled for sale on the secondhand market. This leaves the army with 18 front-line howitzers. In addition, its Multiple-Launch Rocket Systems and the modernized Cheetah self-propelled anti-aircraft guns will also be phased out. One of four Patriot missile batteries will be deactivated.[90]

The Dutch Army (and the Dutch Navy's Marines) is on track to receive new tracked vehicles to replace its YPR 765s, which are up for sale. The new acquisitions include CV9030s, Fenneks, and Bushmasters.[91]

Looking to the future, the Netherlands has identified several new procurement priorities. These include the ability to acquire or support the following:

- digital resilience and cyber operations
- MALE UAV (single system, four aircraft)
- ballistic missile defense
- counter–improvised explosive device (IED)
- Network Enabled Capabilities
- satellite communications (SATCOM)
- psychologocial operations (PsyOps)
- integrated fire support.[92]

---

[90] "Dutch Initiate Defense Cuts," *Defense Technology International*, June 1, 2011.

[91] "Western Europe—Procurement—Netherlands," 2011.

[92] "NL Defense Post-Financial Crisis," 2011.

Cuts in Training and Readiness

The Royal Netherlands Army is facing cuts in training as a result of the defense budget cuts. Fewer vehicles for educational and training purposes are available, and the MoD is well aware of the consequences. As far back as November 2010, Minister of Defense Hans Hillen warned that the proficiency of the mechanized infantry units could no longer be assured from late 2011.[93]

Changes and Elimination of Military Missions

Dutch support for the ISAF was virtually concluded by August 2010. Most of the ground forces have been withdrawn, though four RNLAF F-16s and 120 staff are programmed to remain.[94] The Dutch military will replace its infantry presence in Afghanistan with the *Koninklijke Marechausse* (KM), a separate service of the Dutch Armed Forces equivalent to France's Gendarmerie. These forces work with the Netherlands Ministry of Justice and Ministry of Interior and will play an important role in the integrated police training mission in Kundoz, Afghanistan. The MoD has said that it is focusing on essential operations capabilities because it wants Dutch forces to be more capable in the fields of expeditionary operations, network-centric warfare, new weapons, and unmanned and semi-autonomous systems.[95]

Future Deployability and Sustainability Challenges

Many of the cuts mentioned in the capabilities section will affect the deployability and sustainability of all of the Dutch Armed Forces. Fewer ALQ-131 self-protection jammer pods for the F-16s are now being acquired. In addition, upgrades to the Patriot air defense systems are also delayed. Cougar helicopter engine updates will no longer

---

93 "Western Europe—Army—Netherlands," *Jane's Sentinel Security Assessment*, June 13, 2011.

94 "Western Europe—Air Force—Netherlands," 2011.

95 "Western Europe—Procurement—Netherlands," 2011.

include upgrades that allow operability in hot climates—severely limiting its durability in the Middle East and South Asia.

For the army, supplies of spare parts and factory support for maintenance have decreased as a result of a contract obligation break in 2010. In addition, airmobile infantry battalions, combat support and logistics units, antiaircraft artillery companies, and repair companies are below strength. For instance, *Jane's Sentinel Security Assessment* reports that the material readiness of the Fennek is only at 57 percent.

The Royal Netherlands Navy has also been hit with cuts to its spare equipment and maintenance programs. This will inhibit readiness to deploy. The contraction of the Navy's fleet of ships designed for operations in littoral or confined waters is of particular concern. This capability is in short supply in the Alliance's forces, while demand is growing.

The Netherlands will continue to focus on cooperation with its allies to support its operations. The Dutch will maintain participation in such initiatives as the Benelux defense cooperation (with Netherlands-Belgium naval cooperation being the most mature), the UK/Netherland Amphibious Force, the German-Netherlands Corps headquarters, the European Air Transport Command, and the European Gendarmerie Force.[96]

The Dutch Armed Forces were downsized from 46,330 in 2005 to 40,804 in 2010, a 12 percent reduction for that period; further cuts are foreseen to 2014, which will affect the military's combat readiness and deployability until then. Meanwhile, the defense budget grew by 14 percent over 2005–2009, from €7.67 to €8.73 billion. However, an overall 13 percent spending cut is planned through 2015.

The percentage of GDP spent on defense has remained below the target 2 percent GDP spending mark, at an average of 1.46 percent between 2005 and 2010, fluctuating between 1.36 percent in 2008 to 1.53 percent in 2009 (Figure 2.6).

---

[96] "The Netherlands Defence Organisation After the Credit Crunch: A Smaller Force in a Troubled World," April 19, 2011, memorandum provided to RAND by Royal Netherlands Embassy on July 13, 2011.

Figure 2.6
Dutch Military Personnel and Defense Spending as a Percentage of GDP, 2005–2010

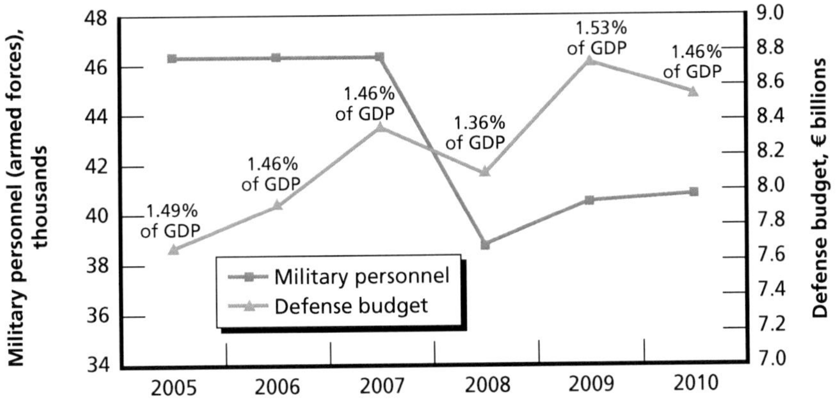

SOURCE: *The Impact of the Financial Crisis on European Defence: Annex*, 2011, p. 56.
RAND *MG1196-2.6*

Poland

Since joining NATO in 1999, Poland has become a vital member of the Alliance, with significant troop contributions and leading roles in Iraq, Afghanistan, and other international missions. While engaged in operational theaters in Europe, Africa, Asia, and the Middle East, the Polish Armed Forces have undergone significant restructuring. In 2008, Poland decided to professionalize its army. It ended conscription and, partly as a result, troop levels have dropped from 180,000 in 1999, when Poland joined NATO, to 100,000 at the end of 2011. In 2009, it adopted an ambitious ten-year modernization plan to replace its aging equipment and increase the interoperability, deployability and sustainability of its military.

Changes in Military Spending

Poland weathered the global economic crisis much better than most European countries and, as a result, it has not only been able to withstand the need to cut its defense budget further, but has increased defense spending in the past several years. While the 2010 budget was implemented in full and without difficulties, Poland's Ministry of National Defense was unable to boost investment in part because of the need to cover the contracts it had renegotiated in 2009.[97]

Poland's economy performed well in 2011. Consequently, experts announced in January 2012 that the defense budget would rise by 7.8 percent in 2012, to $8.79 billion.[98] As of June 2012, the budget was $8.56 billion (29.5 billion in Polish zloty [PLN]), confirming the predicted budget rise.[99] The 2009 forecast figures indicating that the defense budget would rise from PLN 23.8 billion in 2009 to PLN 28 billion in 2013[100] have thus already been superseded by the growth in 2012, and by a further expected growth of 7 percent in 2013.[101] This growth trend in defense expenditure could, however, be reversed if the government were to go ahead with the amendment of the law that earmarks 1.95 percent of the GDP for national defense. In 2010, the Tusk government considered modifying the law so that the budget would average 1.95 percent of GDP over the course of six years, in effect permitting it to spend less than that in any given fiscal year.[102] Such a decision could result in a significant and potentially permanent decrease of Polish defense expenditures, which would be difficult to reverse given that there is little public or political support for defense spending.[103] Such a decision could thus have important consequences for Poland's

---

97 *The Impact of the Financial Crisis on European Defence: Annex*, 2011, pp. 22–25.

98 Christina Mackenzie and Andy Nativi, "Chopping Budgest in Europe," *Aviation Week*, January 5, 2012.

99 Interview with Polish Defense official, June 22, 2012.

100 Hugh Bayley, "Information Document: The Global Financial Crisis and Its Impact on Defense Budgets," 2009 Annual Session Reports, NATO Parliamentary Assembly, November 2009.

101 Interview with Polish Defense official, June 22, 2012.

102 Jaroslaw Adamowski, "Poland's Defense Budget Rises, with Emphasis on Modernization," *Defense News*, September 20, 2010.

103 Sophie Brune, Alistair Cameron, Jean-Pierre Maulny, and Marcin Terlikowski, "Restructuring Europe's Armed Forces in Times of Austerity: The United Kingdom, France, Germany and Poland," Working Paper—Stiftung Wissenschaft und Politik, November 2010.

force-modernization plans. The government, however, has not as yet taken any further steps to amend the law, and there are no plans to make any budget cuts that would affect Poland's 1.95-percent-of-GDP in annual defense spending.[104]

Changes in Military Manpower Levels

Over the course of the past decade, Poland has downsized its armed forces significantly. When Poland joined NATO in 1999, the Polish Armed Forces had 180,000 personnel.[105] In 2008, it decided to professionalize its armed forces, which has led to a very significant reduction in manpower. Poland's last conscript left service in August 2009, and the force strength of its now fully professional armed forces was expected to have grown to 100,000 by the end of 2011; in August 2011, 46,920 served in the army, 7,730 in the navy, 17,000 in the air force, and close to an additional 24,600 served in other services: the Warsaw Garrison Command (2,700), the Military Police (3,400), the Inspectorate for the Armed Forces Support (9,600) and in other units (8,900).[106] A recently established National Reserve Force has 20,000 personnel. An initially low number of 5,000 reserve recruits in 2010 led to the greater allocation of funds for recruitment in 2011.[107]

Poland's special operations forces are now in a separate service in the country's military structure. The branch had approximately 1,500 personnel in 2009, but that number was expected to grow to 3,500 between 2009 and 2012.[108] In 2009, Poland signed a memorandum of understanding that established a strategic partnership between Polish and U.S. special operations commands. The special operatons forces of the two countries have been cooperating extensively, and the United

[104] Interview with Polish defense official, June 22, 2012.

[105] Matthew Day, "Poland Ends Army Conscription," *Daily Telegraph*, August 5, 2008.

[106] "Central Europe and the Baltic States—Armed Forces—Poland," *Jane's Sentinel Security Assessment*, August 23, 2011.

[107] "Central Europe and the Baltic States—Armed Forces—Poland," 2011.

[108] Jim Geramone, "U.S., Poland Sign Special Ops Memo of Understanding," American Foreign Press Service, February 19, 2009.

States has also continued to assist in enabling Poland to become a "fully interoperable special operations forces partner nation by 2014."[109]

The new structure of Poland's armed forces was laid out in the 2009–2012 Defense Plan, signed in May 2009 by Defense Minister Bogdan Klich. However, even though the economic crisis has left Poland fiscally better off than many of its European neighbors, the country decided to overhaul the Ministry of National Defense's spending structure through a reduction in personnel expenses, in particular by cutting civilian jobs by up to 10 percent,[110] with civilians in the three services, civilian guard units, and logistics most affected by the cuts.[111]

Force Structure Cuts

Poland's armed forces have experienced numerous structural reforms since the early 1990s, and the country's participation in NATO and EU operations has acted as a key driver for force development and reorganization.[112] However, the financial crisis did force the Ministry of National Defense to undertake some force structure cuts. In May 2009, Klich signed an annex to the 2009–2012 Defense Plan, designed to restructure Poland's land forces so as to generate an internal structure that would be less costly and more effective. This decision was linked to the budget drop from the planned PLN 24.5 billion to PLN 22.6 billion, and is regarded as a decision "bypassing" Poland's 2009–2018 Defense Plan. The annex envisioned that the forces would be restructured as follows:[113]

---

[109] "Fact Sheet: U.S.-Poland Bilateral Defense Cooperation," Office of the Press Secretary, The White House, May 28, 2011.

[110] Christian Mölling and Sophie-Charlotte Brune, *The Impact of the Financial Crisis on European Defence*, Brussels: Directorate-General for External Policies of the Union—Policy Department, European Parliament, Ref: EP/EXPO/B/SEDE/FWC/2009-01/Lot6/09, April 2011.

[111] *The Impact of the Financial Crisis on European Defence: Annex*, 2011, pp. 22–25.

[112] "Central Europe and the Baltic States—Armed Forces—Poland," 2011.

[113] "Central Europe and the Baltic States—Army—Poland," *Jane's Sentinel Security Assessment*, August 23, 2011.

- The Land Forces will lose one of their four divisional headquarters; the units under the 1st Mechanised Division Headquarters in Legionowo are to be reallocated to three other headquarters, primarily to the 16th Mechanized Division in Elblag.
- The 6th Air Assault Brigade is to be reorganized from 2010 into an airborne (parachute) brigade to increase its mobility, while two sapper, one engineering, and two Nuclear, Biological, and Chemical (NBC) regiments are to remain within the land forces structure.
- A new Land Forces Aviation Brigade was established in January 2012, with squadrons of helicopters located in Inowroclaw and Pruszcz Gdanski and a UAV squadron to be based in Miroslawiec.
- All artillery assets will be concentrated in three artillery regiments, while low-level air-defense assets will form three regiments. These units are likely to continue to use the 9K33 OSA-AKM (SA-8) and 2K12 Kub-M (SA-6) surface-to-air missile systems beyond 2016.[114]

Additional force structure decisions that were taken are as follows:[115]

- The Armed Forces' Operational HQ—a joint services headquarters that is in charge of all armed forces missions—will remain in Warsaw.
- Poland's army will lose one divisional HQ—the 1st Mechanized Division HQ—and will divide all mechanized and armored combat brigades around the remaining three HQs.

In 2009, Poland also decided to replace its air force's brigade structure with aviation wing organizations, including one that is dedicated to training. It is expected that further reorganization will follow. By 2020, the Ministry of National Defense wants to have an air force structure in place that will be based on "two groups of units conduct-

114 "Central Europe and the Baltic States—Army—Poland," 2011.

115 "Central Europe and the Baltic States—Army—Poland," 2011.

ing operational and non-operational missions, supported by a flat and responsive two-level command system."[116]

Changes in Modernization Plans

Poland is currently undergoing a "deep transformation" that involves three key elements: professionalization of the armed forces, administrative reforms, and technical modernization, which aims at replacing aging post-Soviet equipment and increasing of the level of the sustainability, interoperability, and deployability of the armed forces.[117]

In October 2009, the Polish government approved a four-year development program for the armed forces[118] and announced an ambitious 14-point modernization plan, which includes a PLN 30.5 billion ($10.7 billion) procurement plan for the period 2009–2018; by 2012 it intends to allocate circa PLN 5 billion per annum for procurement purposes, which amounts to 5 percent more than was spent over the period 2006–2009.[119] Warsaw's plan includes the following areas and elements:[120]

- air defense
- helicopters
- naval procurement and life extensions, particularly frigates and submarines
- C4ISR
- UAVs
- simulators and training devices
- Lead-in Fighter Trainer (LIFT) aircraft and training infrastructure
- Tytan advanced individual combat systems (the Polish future soldier program)

---

[116] "Central Europe and the Baltic States—Navy—Poland," *Jane's Sentinel Security Assessment*, October 26, 2011.

[117] Brune et al., 2010.

[118] *The Impact of the Financial Crisis on European Defence: Annex*, 2011, pp. 22–25.

[119] "Central Europe and the Baltic States—Procurement—Poland," *Jane's Sentinel Security Assessment*, November 4, 2011.

[120] "Central Europe and the Baltic States—Procurement—Poland," 2011.

- PZL M28 Bryza STOL transport aircraft
- Rosomak wheeled armored vehicles
- Spike anti-tank weapon systems
- WR-40 Langusta extended-range multiple rocket launchers (MRLs)
- WR-300 Homar medium- and long-range MRLs
- 155mm self-propelled howitzers (tracked Krab and wheeled Kryl systems).

This modernization program involves a number of large procurement projects, some of which were set to be concluded in the relatively short time span of three to four years, such as the purchase of 16 fighter-jet trainers, 48 Patria/Rosomak wheeled armored vehicles, and 26 support helicopters (down from the original planned minimum of 51). Poland also has very ambitious procurement plans for the period after 2018, such as the comprehensive improvements of its C4ISR capabilities and the acquisition of a new aerial and missile defense system.[121] However, there are no plans to procure new combat aircraft before 2018, and the air force is not going to receive its long-awaited two MALE UAV systems prior to that year.[122] As part of its modernization efforts, Poland also plans to withdraw substantial numbers of old equipment, such as dozens of its Sukhoi Su-22 bombers and hundreds of its Soviet-era T-72 tanks.[123] However, such withdrawals are contingent on procurements going ahead as planned; should there be any delays, it is likely that the life of old equipment will be extended.[124]

It is clear, though, that some branches of the military will begin to lose capabilities if no new acquisitions are made by 2018. While the land forces have new eqipment and are doing well in that respect because of Poland's involvement in Iraq and Afghanistan, Poland's navy is in the worst shape of all its military branches, with no replacements for its aging equipment and with the cancellation of the Gawron

---

[121] *The Impact of the Financial Crisis on European Defence: Annex*, 2011, pp. 22–25.

[122] "Central Europe and the Baltic States—Procurement—Poland," 2011.

[123] "Central Europe and the Baltic States—Procurement—Poland," 2011.

[124] "Central Europe and the Baltic States—Procurement—Poland," 2011.

Corvette warship project. Aviation is also struggling with a lack of helicopters. There is some indication, though, that Poland's priorities after Afghanistan may potentially shift to its ailing navy.[125] All modernization plans are, however, contingent on Poland's ability to keep its defense budget at 1.95 percent of GDP.[126]

Elimination of an Important Capability

Full details of the specific programs that were affected by the budgetary cuts in 2009 have not been released to date. Nevertheless, available data indicates that the number of PZL Mielec M-28 aircraft has been cut: In April 2011, Poland received the first of eight M-28 aircraft, four less than the 12 it had originally ordered. The figure for the helicopters is even more substantial: Poland had originally planned to order a minimum of 51, but has now settled on acquiring only 26 tactical transport, combat support, VIP, antisubmarine warfare (ASW), and SAR helicopters, which will be delivered by 2018 for circa PLN 6.5 billion and will be issued to the land forces, navy, and the special forces. And while the land forces are retiring hundreds of their tanks, Poland's procurement plans until 2018 do not include the purchase of new MBTs, even though such a requirement had been indicated by both defense ministry and military officials. This could leave Poland's armed forces without significant MBT capabilities, especially since there are also no current plans to upgrade the 128 Leopard 2A4 MBTs acquired from Germany, even though the tanks require significant investment.[127]

Cuts in Training and Readiness

The budget cut in 2009 led to the suspension of field exercises so that maintenance and training costs could be reduced.[128] The budget increase over the past two years will mean, though, that Poland's readiness will not be affected significantly by the economic crisis in Europe.

---

125 Interview with Polish defense official, June 22, 2012.

126 Brune et al., 2010.

127 "Central Europe and the Baltic States—Procurement—Poland," 2011.

128 *The Impact of the Financial Crisis on European Defence: Annex*, 2011, pp. 22–25.

In line with NATO's objectives and those of the EU's Common Security and Defense Policy, the basic levels of readiness in the Polish Armed Forces include the following:[129]

- high-readiness forces ready within 90 days and NATO Response Forces or EU Rapid Response Forces ready between five and 30 days
- low-readiness forces ready within 365 days or for the initial rotation of high-readiness forces, ready by up to six months
- long-term build-up forces ready for engagement at first within 365 days, to be developed by mobilization.[130]

In the first half of 2010, Poland was ready to undertake Common Security and Defense Policy missions through its participation in one of the EU's battlegroups, which included Germany, Slovakia, Lithuania, and Latvia. Furthermore, Poland agreed to join France and Germany as part of the Weimar Battlegroup and was designated to be the lead nation of this configuration, which is set to serve in the first half of 2013.[131] Poland has also taken the lead in developing the Visegrad Battlegroup, which will be composed of the forces from a number of Central European countries—Hungary, Slovakia, and the Czech Republic—and will be deployable in 2016.[132] Poland's enhanced role and leadership in these battlegroup formations signals that the country's readiness to participate in international missions has not been undermined by austerity measures.

Changes and Elimination of Military Missions

Poland has contributed significantly to a number of NATO and EU operations, as well as numerous UN missions. It still maintains a battalion in NATO's Kosovo Force (KFOR) and has been one of the lead-

---

[129] "Central Europe and the Baltic States—Navy—Poland," 2011.

[130] "Central Europe and the Baltic States—Navy—Poland," 2011.

[131] "World Armies—Poland," *Jane's World Armies*, December 19, 2011.

[132] Cat Contigugulia, "ČR, Poland Talk Military Alliance: Top Generals Convene Meeting on Pooling of Resources amid Cuts," *Prague Post*, October 19, 2011.

ing contributors to ISAF in Afghanistan.[133] Polish soldiers served in Operation Enduring Freedom in Afghanistan and Operation Iraqi Freedom, and they also serve in NATO's training mission in Iraq.[134] Polish ships participate in NATO's Operation Active Endeavour in the Mediterranean, and, in 2010, Poland took part in NATO's air policing mission designed to protect the Baltic countries.[135] Overall, the years of experience that Polish soldiers have had in Iraq and Afghanistan, including successful battle operations, have served to increase NATO's combat power.[136]

The budget cuts in 2009 forced Poland to withdraw its deployment with the United Nations Disengagement Observer Force (UNDOF) in Syria, so that it could focus more on NATO and EU missions.[137] It also withdrew from Lebanon (UNIFIL) and Chad (MINURCAT), so that it would be able to shift more troops to Afghanistan.[138] President Bronislaw Komorowski promised during his presidential campaign in 2010 that he would withdraw the Polish ISAF contingent by 2012.[139] However, Poland will be able to fully withdraw only when it completes its NATO obligation of training Afghan security forces and ridding Ghazhni Province, where the Polish contingent is based, of the Taliban.[140] In June 2011, Deputy Defense Minister Czeslaw Piatas confirmed the government's decision to begin a partial drawdown process during the subsequent rotation of soldiers, which was scheduled for October 2011.[141] While the Ministry of National Defense had not announced by the end of 2011 the precise number of soldiers that would

---

[133] U.S. Department of State, Bureau of European and Eurasian Affairs, "Background Notes—Poland," August 30, 2011.

[134] U.S. Department of State, Bureau of European and Eurasian Affairs, 2011.

[135] *The Impact of the Financial Crisis on European Defence: Annex*, 2011, pp. 22–25.

[136] "World Armies—Poland," 2011.

[137] "World Armies—Poland," 2011.

[138] *The Impact of the Financial Crisis on European Defence: Annex*, 2011, pp. 22–25.

[139] *The Impact of the Financial Crisis on European Defence: Annex*, 2011, pp. 22–25.

[140] "World Armies—Poland," 2011.

[141] "World Armies—Poland," 2011.

leave the mission, army sources had said that it could be 5–7 percent of the near 2,600 troops based in Ghazni Province and of the 300-person strategic reserve based in Poland.[142]

Poland's planned withdrawal from Afghanistan will take place in three phases: During phase one, which will last until the end of October 2012, the current force strength of 2,500 soldiers will remain in theater, and 200 soldiers will remain in reserve in Poland. Phase two, from October 2012 until October 2013, will see a reduction of force strength to 1,800 in theater if circumstances allow it, and an increase of deployable reserves in Poland to 400; this phase would potentially also see the transfer of the city of Ghazni and districts with high levels of stability to the authority of the Afghan National Security Forces (ANSF). And phase three, from October 2013 until approximately the end of 2014, will see the troop nubers reduced to 1,000 in theater and 200 deployable reserves in Poland, with activities focusing mainly on intense training and mentoring of the ANSF and a transfer of the remaining districts to the authority of the ANSF. A full withdrawal is planned by the end of 2014.[143] By January 2015, Poland plans to have no more operational troops in Afghanistan, but to continue with military training and advising. It also plans to provide circa $20 million per year to the ANSF; however, Poland will first have to determine how it can do so in a lawful manner, since the law does not currently allow Poland to support foreign forces.[144]

Future Deployability and Sustainability Challenges

Poland's current "level of ambition" when it comes to deployment remains classified; experts, however, hold that it includes "deployment based on different levels of mission intensity, sustainability, requirements and concurrency" and that the limit of Poland's sustainable capacity lies at 4,000, a little over half the number that Germany is

---

142 "World Armies—Poland," 2011.

143 Ministerstwo Obrony Narodowej, "Podstawowe Informacje o Budzecie Resotru Obrony Narodowej na 2012 R," Department Budzetowy, Warsawa, Marzec, 2012 R.

144 Interview with Polish defense official, June 22, 2012.

able to deploy and sustain.[145] However, as the Polish Armed Forces are being transformed into a professional army, the share of the forces that are deployable and sustainable is gradually increasing.[146] Currently, the armed forces are organized in a way that enables soldiers to stay in the field for at least six-month rotations; however, unless operational needs require an exception, soldiers are not allowed to participate in back-to-back rotations and must take a break of one year between tours of duty.[147]

Poland participates in NATO's Strategic Airlift Capability program and is one of ten states able to use the C-17 *Globemaster* III strategic transport aircraft for up to 45 hours per year, which amounts to circa six flights between Poland and Kabul. Unlike Italy, it has been able to retain its membership in the program, which will enable it to continue to deploy personnel and oversized cargo to operational theaters.[148] Poland's plan for future deployable forces is to have two brigade combat teams by 2015–2016, with an end strength of circa 2,500–3,000 soldiers each, capable of participating in major land operations; in addition, it plans to have two battalions for low-intensity conflict.[149]

While troop numbers have dropped by 29 percent from 140,000 in 2007 to 100,000 in 2010, Poland's defense budget has grown by over 50 percent between 2005 and 2010, despite the economic downturn. The budget crisis of 2009 put only a temporary damper on Poland's defense spending and budget growth. Although its expenditure is small in comparison to that of other European allies, Poland carries its required weight and is one of the few members that spends consistently close to the desired amount of 2 percent of GDP on defense (Figure 2.7).

---

145 *The Impact of the Financial Crisis on European Defence: Annex*, 2011, pp. 22–25.

146 "World Armies—Poland," 2011.

147 "World Armies—Poland," 2011.

148 "Central Europe and the Baltic States—Armed Forces—Poland," 2011.

149 Interview with Polish defense official, June 22, 2012.

Figure 2.7
Polish Military Personnel and Defense Spending as a Percentage of GDP, 2005–2010

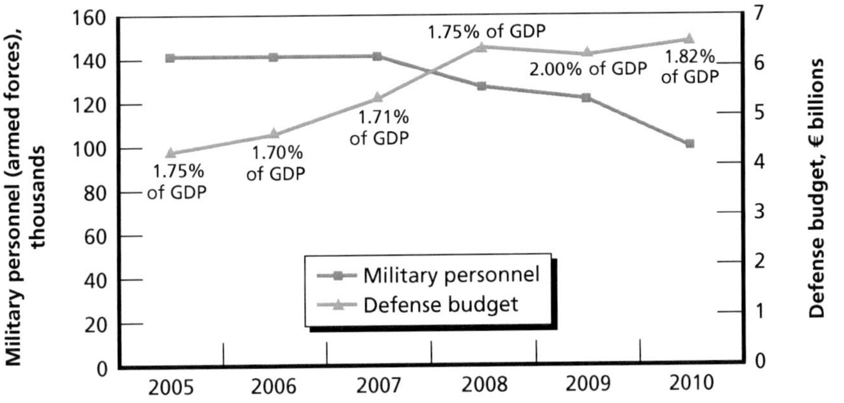

SOURCE: *The Impact of the Financial Crisis on European Defence: Annex*, 2011, p. 22.
RAND *MG1196-2.7*

Future Prospects

There has been a broad trend in Europe toward the reduction of troop numbers (Figure 2.8), which has resulted in part from the end of conscription and the professionalization of the armed forces in a number of European countries, and in part by budget cuts related to the financial crisis. Significant troop cuts were undertaken in the United Kingdom, Germany, Poland, and Spain. While the reduced number of British soldiers is going to have a negative and serious impact on NATO's overall combat power, the fact that only 7,000 of Germany's troops and 4,000 of Poland's troops are readily deployable renders these troop reductions less significant. In fact, as German and Polish forces become more professional, more are likely to become deployable. In the case of Germany, though, politics will continue to play an important part in its willingness to undertake expeditionary missions.

The financial crisis has had a negative impact on defense budgets across Europe, and significant budget cuts were made in 2009 in the UK, France, and Spain, with Italy and Poland also experiencing cuts. Germany and the Netherlands stand out since their budgets actually

Figure 2.8
Military Personnel (Armed Forces) of Key NATO Allies, 2005–2010

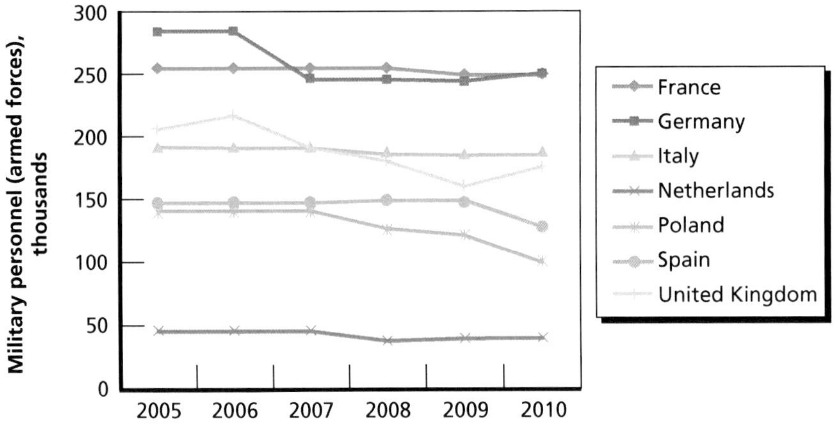

SOURCE: *The Impact of the Financial Crisis on European Defence: Annex*, 2011.
RAND *MG1196-2.8*

increased amidst the crisis, in real numbers and as a percentage of GDP, reflecting economies that did better than those of their neighbors. Further budget cuts, however, foreseen for the period 2012–2014 in Germany will result in an €8 billion decline from the current €31 billion. This would amount to one of the largest declines in defense spending in Europe—a total of 25 percent, a significantly larger percentage than the 7.5 percent cuts announced by the UK and the 13 percent cuts the Netherlands plans to undertake till 2015.

Given the poor state of the economy in Spain, further cuts can also be expected there, and the pressure to reduce public debt in Italy is also likely to lead to further cuts in 2013. While no major cuts are expected for France to 2014, Poland stands out as the only country that has managed to actually increase its budget, by 7 percentage points in 2011 and with a similar rise expected for 2012; this is a significant increase at a time of austerity measures across Europe. Overall, the budget cuts in Europe will result in a decrease of the combat readiness and deployability of the NATO members in this study until at least the middle of the decade. But since any operational budget cuts would increase the risks to the troops serving in Afghanistan under these countries' flags, such budgets may not in fact be implemented until the troops start to withdraw in significant numbers.

While Poland has the smallest defense budget of the countries in this study, it has the third-largest as percentage of GDP, after the UK and France (Figure 2.9). It consistently spends close to the 2 percent level desired by NATO, outperforming France in 2008, 2009, and 2010. Of those countries included in this study, the worst performers on this scale are Italy and Spain, which have spent on average less than 1 percent of GDP on defense, with Spain averaging 0.75 percent between 2005 and 2010. While the percentage of GDP spent on defense rose for the UK, France, Germany, the Netherlands, and Poland during the worst year to affect budgets—2009—it dropped slightly for Italy and Spain. It is unclear how future budget cuts will affect the percentage of GDP that countries spend on defense. However, given that the figures have been relatively stable other than for the UK, which has seen a rise by more than 1 percentage point between 2007 and 2009, it is unlikely that we will witness significant changes—unless the economy takes a turn for the worse once again.

Figure 2.9
Defense Budget of Key NATO Allies as a Percentage of GDP, 2005–2010

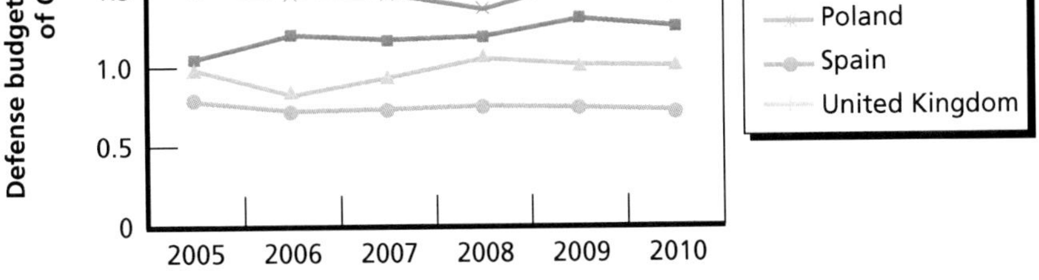

SOURCE: *The Impact of the Financial Crisis on European Defence: Annex*, 2011.
RAND *MG1196-2.9*

CHAPTER THREE

NATO Europe's Capability for Defense and Power Projection in the Coming Decade

The previous chapter examined the impact of planned austerity measures on the force posture of key NATO allies. This chapter assesses the impact of planned austerity measures on NATO Europe's military ability to carry out five different missions: (1) defense of NATO territory (e.g., protecting the eastern members of NATO; (2) missions in NATO's immediate neighborhood (e.g., the Mediterranean littoral); (3) power-projection missions in more distant regions (e.g., the Persian Gulf); (4) long-range operations with small conventional forces (e.g., peacekeeping in Africa); and (5) long-range SOF (counterterrorism and COIN) operations.

Defense of NATO Territory

Article V (collective defense) is a core NATO mission. NATO has long agreed that the Article V threats to its members are changing in nature, and has sought to adapt its Strategic Concept and plans accordingly. There is a widespread view within NATO that the specter of a classic invasion threat from any neighboring country, such as a resurgent Russia, has receded and that a major threat is unlikely to reemerge for a decade or more. However, some East European members, particularly the Baltic States, Poland, and Romania, continue to be concerned about the modernization of Russian military capability and the willingness of Moscow to use force in areas where it has strong national interests, particularly in the post-Soviet space.[1] Given these concerns, it may be worth considering what NATO's capabilities for defense against this threat are going to be in the future.

This section examines NATO Europe's role and ability to contribute to the defense of East European territory against an emerging military threat from Russia, however unlikley that threat may appear at the moment. Such an attack would constitute a classic Article V security threat and provoke a response involving U.S. forces. As will be discussed in greater detail below, only Germany, France, and the UK will have forces that could be moved relatively quickly by air, sea, and ground lift to a menaced eastern periphery of NATO.[2] Poland and/or Romania will provide their multi-brigade national defense forces if threatened.[3] The Baltic States, however, will have no meaningful self-defense capability against even the current Russian Armed Forces. U.S. forces in Europe participating in such a deterrent and/or combat operation would likely be a mix of light, medium, and heavy brigades, U.S. Air Forces in Europe (USAFE) air units, and their associated air,

---

[1] At the present time, the prospect of a rapidly emerging military threat from Russia is remote, since the Russian Armed Forces have not undergone major reforms to transform into an operationally ready, high-technology-enabled expeditionary force. For an analysis of the failure of the Russian military to professionalize its forces, see Rod Thornton, *Military Modernization and the Russian Ground Forces*, Carlisle, Pa.: Strategic Studies Institute, 2011. Russian ground forces continue to rely on drafted recruits with one-year terms of service that drastically reduce the readiness of these forces. NATO would have substantial strategic warning of such a potentially menacing transformation of the Russian Armed Forces. For a comprehensive analysis of Russian modernization prospects, see Olga Oliker, Keith Crane, Lowell H. Schwartz, and Catherine Yusupov, *Russian Foreign Policy Sources and Implications*, Santa Monica, Calif.: RAND Corporation, MG-768-AF, 2009.

[2] In this hypothetical, future scenario, German forces will be able to rely primarily on the regional road and rail nets to move their rapid response forces as part of a NATO flexible deterrent option. Only France and Germany could each provide two heavy brigades by the end of this decade. The operational deployment of these heavy units will require the employment of the German and French freight rail system, since neither will retain, even in reserve formations, a fleet of heavy equipment transporters.

[3] Poland is likely to retain several armored mechanized ("heavy") brigades. By the post-2015 timeframe, the Polish forces may have the largest heavy force outside of Turkey. Romania will have a far less capable national defense capacity.

naval, and ISR capability.[4] If the political-military crisis was severe, the United States could provide additional reinforcement by air and sea that would likely be a mix of light, medium, and heavy brigades drawn from the U.S. East and Gulf coasts. In turn, these land forces would follow a likely rapid response by the USAF and U.S. Navy to provide additional air and ISR support. The defense of Poland and/or Romania would depend in part on the willingness of Belarus and Ukraine to provide Russian troops free passage to the theater of operations. In conclusion, NATO's defense capabilities (i.e., including U.S. forces) are more than adequate to deter a classic Article V contingency. The West would have sufficient warning of any Russian military build-up to take the necessary countermeasure to deter an attack.[5]

More plausible in the near and medium future are the emergence of "unconventional" threats to NATO by states or nonstate groups. These include terrorist threats, threats posed by long-range ballistic

---

4 This assumes that the recently reduced U.S. peacetime military presence in NATO Europe will stay at the level of two permanently based brigade combat teams (BCTs), a Stryker motorized cavalry, and an airborne brigade after the demobilization of the two heavy BCTs based in Europe. In the future, heavy BCTs in the contiguous United States will participate in regular training exercises in the region. USAFE, the peacetime air component of U.S. European Command, will be scaled back with the withdrawal of two combat squadrons from Germany and one from Italy. The bulk of personnel cuts appear to fall on U.S. Army forces and will include the demobilization of the V Corps with its associated personnel. Noteworthy is the permanent deployment of four Aegis ballistic missile defense–capable warships to their new homeport in Rota, Spain. See Michelle Tan and Richard Sandza, "European Pullout Plan to move 2 BCTs and up to 10,000 Soldiers Could Start in October," *Army Times*, January 23, 2012; and Julian E. Barnes, "U.S. to Cut Europe Forces in Remake," *Wall Street Journal*, February 17, 2012.

5 Much lower combat force density will put a premium on aerospace power supremacy, as confirmed by the recent Libyan intervention to insure NATO forces can respond to a rapidly emerging future military threat from Russia. This appreciation of the fundamental change in the military and technological balance in the Baltic region was articulated by Swedish defense planners during and after a December 1, 2011, conference on the future of U.S. European Command and its relationship with NATO. In any hypothetical crisis/conflict between the Baltic states and the Russian Federation, any NATO military response, either in the form of a flexible deterrent option or outright combat, would involve the employment of combat air power and ISR assets to gain local air dominance to support a small ground expeditionary force delivered by air and sea. For a candid view of possible military conflict in the Baltic region, see Bo Hugemark, *Friends in Need: Toward a Swedish Strategy of Solidarity with Her Neighbours*, Stockholm: Royal Swedish Academy of War Science, 2012.

missiles, threats through cyberspace, and threats posed by criminal organizations.

There is the well-understood strategic threat that continues as the menace of radical Islam and/or its doppelganger: radical nationalism and racism. Another possible strategic threat is an attack against critical national infrastructures through cyberspace.[6] Within the NATO nations, there may emerge a wide difference of opinion whether the threshold of damage caused by cyber attacks does or does not constitute an act of war. Also, there may be major differences in view as to whether a credible deterrent, e.g., a counterattack response, is or is not feasible, given the difficulty of timely and reliable attribution of the attacking source.[7]

Classic conventional military forces are modestly relevant to this strategic threat, although they may play an important role in dealing with the damage response and recovery to a terrorist event, especially if damage is of a weapon-of-mass-destruction magnitude. The most important military capabilities in this regard are combat service support forces, such as engineering, medical, and nuclear, biological, and chemical (NBC) decontamination and reconstruction units. Many of these capabilities are being cut back as budgets shrink, especially in the more capable NATO Europe militaries, to protect what is left of their combat forces.

Finally, there is the possible emergence of a nuclear threat from Iran and other possible proliferators in the Greater Middle East that may emerge after an Iranian nuclear breakout scenario.[8] By the end of the decade, Iran may have an operational first-generation nuclear arse-

---

[6] For a discussion of the emerging cyber threats to national critical infrastructures, see David C. Nicol, "Hacking the Lights Out: Computer Viruses Have Taken Out Hardened Industrial Control Systems—The Electric Power Grid May Be Next," *Scientific American*, July 2011.

[7] For a discussion of this major policy challenge for NATO, see Jeffrey Carr, "What Is Cyberwar? The Defense Community Can't Figure out How to Define It," *Slate*, August 12, 2011.

[8] For a discussion of Iran's near-term nuclear weapon breakout capabilities see Gregory S. Jones, "An In-Depth Examination of Iran's Centrifuge Enrichment Program and Its Efforts to Acquire Nuclear Weapons," *Nonproliferation Policy Education Center*, August 9, 2011.

nal equipped with solid-propellant intermediate-range ballistic missiles capable of threatening the major capitals of Europe.[9] More uncertain is whether Iran will deploy medium- and intermediate-range ballistic missiles equipped with precision-guided non-nuclear warheads. As will be discussed below, there is a far higher prospect that a number of states in the Greater Middle East, including Iran, may acquire shorter-range precision-guided missiles as part of an effort to build more effective anti-access/area denial (A2/AD) capabilities.[10]

The military response to this long-range missile threat will require investment in aerospace defenses, counterforce and ISR, and the maintenance of the trilateral nuclear deterrent forces of the United States, France, and the UK. Aerospace defense is part of the Lisbon Ten set of NATO investment initiatives.[11] At the present time, the only strategic ballistic missile defense program under way with respect to Europe is the planned U.S.-funded deployment of U.S. naval and land-based units equipped with an advanced version of the Standard Missile-3 armed with an exo-atmospheric hit-to-kill (HTK) interceptor.[12] Currently, this program is diplomatically tied up in the ongoing negotiations with the Russian Federation as to whether such a deployment will be coupled directly or indirectly with a proposed Russian theater missile defense capability.

As for NATO Europe, indigenous missile defense programs are developing at a modest pace. At present, only the next-generation air

---

9 For an authoritative public forecast of Iranian ballistic missile developments, specifically its long-range solid propellant programs, see "Iran's Ballistic Missile Capabilities—A Net Assessment," *IISS Strategic Dossier*, London: International Institute for Strategic Studies, 2010.

10 The source of these long-range precision guided missiles may include China, Russia, and the global arms market. Also, see Robin Hughes, "North Korea Aiding Syria to Upgrade Scud D Capability," *International Defence Review*, June 26, 2012.

11 See "NATO 2020: Assured Security; Dynamic Engagement—Analysis and Recommendations of the Group of Experts on a New Strategic Concept for NATO," NATO Public Diplomacy Division, May 17, 2010, written in preparation for the NATO Summit at Lisbon, November 2010.

12 For a description of the Obama administration's "phased adaptive approach" to European missile defense, see "SM-3 Antimissile System Receives Key Backing at Pentagon," *Global Security Newswire*, August 8, 2011.

and missile defense destroyers will have a capacity to employ terminal missile interceptors. Further, these ship programs are being cut back by the more advanced militaries.[13] Over time, the adequacy of this investment in strategic missile defense will be judged by the expected performance of those defenses against specific and evolving medium- and long-range missile threats that may emerge out of the Greater Middle East.

Missions in NATO's Immediate Neighborhood

Following the planned defense cuts, only four NATO European members will have the military capacity to conduct medium-sized expeditionary operations in the near abroad: France, the UK, Italy, and Germany. Depending on the nature of the political military crisis and its location, Spain and possibly Turkey may play a military role. In theory, the first four countries could make available their expeditionary force. That could involve the deployment of three to six brigades and their supporting air and naval forces. After the planned cuts, both France and the UK will maintain the equivalent of two amphibious brigade combat teams, and Italy will have a large battalion-sized amphibious force and appropriate amphibious ships. All four will have the equivalent of one or two brigades each to be used as follow-on and/or exploitation forces. However, given current reservations in German public opinion about German participation in peace enforcement operations beyond Europe's borders, German leaders may be reluctant to deploy the Bundeswehr to combat operations in the Mediterranean region.

[13] The deployment of a next-generation land-based air defense with a terminal ballistic missile defense capability has suffered a major, or even fatal, setback with the United States and Germany withdrawing from the MEADS program. Only Italy remains as the original member of the trilateral program, and it may demand repayment from the United States for its portion of its investment (author interviews in Rome, July 25, 2011). For discussion about whether components of the MEADS system will be procured as a compromise outcome, see Daniel Wasserbly, "US Looks to Salvage MEADS Components," *International Defense Review*, August 25, 2011. As a result of U.S. Senate intervention, the MEADS program has survived the budgetary knife for another year, with its fate in the FY13 defense budget remaining uncertain.

After the currently planned cuts, the British Army will have one heavy brigade, while France will have only the equivalent of two heavy brigades ("cavalry units") available for this type of operation. Germany will maintain two heavy (armored/mechanized) brigades. Italy and Spain might provide the equivalent of one light, medium, or heavy BCT for this type of operation as additional reinforcements. If Turkey agreed to provide direct military assistance—by no means a given—it might make available one or more heavy brigades.[14] In all cases, to deploy these forces would require an all-out effort to employ the air and sealift assets of NATO Europe.

If the Mediterranean littoral members of the Alliance support this operation in a similar way as they supported the 2011 NATO military operation against Libya, there will likely not be the critical need for a large-deck conventional takeoff and landing (CTOL)–capable aircraft carrier. Fighter-bombers, tankers, and ISR aircraft will be able to take advantage of nearby military airfields.[15] A CTOL-capable aircraft carrier will be very valuable if there is the need for responsive CAS operations from close distances to the target, but these missions might be supplied by large-deck amphibious ships that operate armed helicopters. The British, Italian, and Spanish carriers equipped with the STOVL Joint Strike Fighter will be quite helpful in this regard.[16] As the Libyan military operation suggests, additional key enablers will include the following:

---

[14] As noted, Turkey and Poland may retain the largest heavy force postures in NATO after 2015.

[15] This assumes that the key NATO littoral states, especially Italy, retain their airbase infrastructure to support future littoral operations.

[16] Currently, Italy and Spain operate a small number of the U.S. Marine Corps version of the AV-8B Harrier. Italy hopes to replace this STOVL fighter-bomber with the supersonic F-35B. At present, all models of the Joint Strike Fighter, including the F-35B, will go into limited production at the end of the decade. See Office of the Under Secretary of Defense (Comptroller)/Chief Financial Officer, *Overview, Fiscal Year 2013 Budget Request*, Washington, D.C., February 2012. On the other hand, there is the prospect that the F-35B may be cancelled by the U.S. DoD due to persistent developmental problems and/or as a cost-saving measure to the overall F-35 program. See Bill Sweetman, "Under Fire—Navy Study Looks at Killing One Joint Strike Fighter Version," *Aviation Week & Space Technology*, August 29, 2011.

- sufficient ISR platforms to provide persistent and survivable intelligence and targeting support over important portions of the battlefield
- sufficient armed UAVs to provide persistent air reconnaissance and CAS to maneuvering NATO ground forces
- sufficient suppression of enemy air defense (SEAD) capability, if only to gain local aerial supremacy over the battlefield
- adequate missile defense capability, depending on the level of threat
- sufficient sea mine countermeasure capability to allow amphibious operations to be affected in a militarily decisive manner[17]
- sufficient maritime surveillance and attack capability to defeat the surface and subsurface naval forces of the targeted country
- enough amphibious lift to affect a two-brigade amphibious assault
- sufficient airlift to affect a brigade-sized or larger airborne assault
- sufficient sealift (military and commercial) to deploy and sustain three to five medium and heavy brigades during the exploitation phase
- precision-guided munitions (PGMs) to conduct a multi-month campaign of high tempo.[18]

The Libya operation revealed major deficiencies in NATO Europe's capacity to conduct a protracted air campaign without significant U.S. ISR, tanker, and SEAD support. Our analysis suggests that it is unlikely that NATO Europe will have much improved ISR and SEAD support in the foreseeable future. The UK plans to demobilize much of its aerial ground-oriented ISR capability with the demobilization of the Nimrod R-1 SIGINT and Sentinel airborne radar systems.

---

[17] NATO Europe's mine countermeasure capability continues to shrink. See Chapter Two for details.

[18] The robustness of the NATO European PGM stocks will be an important indicator of their autonomous capacity to conduct any future medium-sized expeditionary operation. The Libyan operation revealed that the UK was running short and had to rely on German and U.S. supplies, since its PGMs were not compatible with the French munitions stocks. See Jon Rosamond, "Europe Takes the Strain on Operation 'United Protector,'" *Jane's Navy International*, July/August 2011.

France has a modest airborne SIGINT capability of a small Transal C-160 and Atlantic antisubmarine warfare aircraft fleets. The touted replacement for this capability is the Alliance Ground Surveillance (AGS) system.[19] The AGS program is in serious trouble due to the decision by Canada to drop out, and the French have expressed reservations about the program's political and operational viability as a jointly developed and deployed NATO European project.[20]

Aside from the German decision to procure as a national program a small fleet of Global Hawk UAVs as SIGINT collectors, NATO Europe does not have a coherent, much less a robust, program to develop significant non-U.S. capabilities in this regard. Neither the UK nor France has a stand-alone SEAD capability. Germany's small fleet of specially modified Tornados represents the only independent European SEAD capability. That capability will likely expire with the full demobilization of the German Tornado fleet by the end of the decade, or even sooner. The NATO Airborne Warning and Control System (AWACS) fleet will remain fully operational during the decade, although there is no program of record as follow-on.

Finally, the NATO Europe tanker capability may improve, if only modestly. During the Libyan operation, the Italian Air Force provided most of the European SEAD capability, due to the absence of the German Luftwaffe.

It is not possible to know the adequacy or inadequacy of NATO ground forces during this type of operation since they were not tested during the Libyan operation. It is noteworthy that the British and French armies will be equipped primarily with a range of medium-

---

[19] Originally, the AGS was to consist of a mix of Global Hawk RQ-4 UAVs and AB-321 equipped with ground surveillance radars and other sensors. In 2007, the AB-321 portion of the program was canceled. Only six Global Hawks with a wide array of ground surveillance sensors remain as the "core" AGS capability. Current public reports suggest the program may be scaled backed to four UAVs that would allow the maintenance of a single surveillance orbit over an operational area of interest. Even this program is at risk with the recent decision by Canada to drop out for cost reasons.

[20] At the present time, the French are resisting making funds available for the AGS Common Operating Fund, even if the system is built. Author interviews in Paris, July 21, 2011.

weight tracked and wheeled AFVs.[21] Most of the British Army's MBT fleet and much of its heavy self-propelled artillery will have been demobilized. The French, Italian, and German ground forces will each keep the equivalent of two heavy (armored mechanized) brigades equipped with MBTs and infantry fighting vehicles. In the case of Italy, the present focus on units deploying to Afghanistan means that the army's heavy armored units are at a low state of readiness and would require considerable time to be ready to fight—probably several months of warning.[22] The planning presumption is that future MBT and heavy armor threats will be dealt with through the use of fixed- and rotary-wing aircraft armed with PGMs.

Additionally, several Mediterranean littoral states may acquire a new generation of long-range precision-guided ballistic and cruise missiles. Syria already appears to have developed and deployed a precision guided short-range ballistic missile, the M600, with Iranian and possible Chinese clandestine assistance.[23]

In addition to acquiring large arsenals of man-portable or light mobile PGMs, over the next decade, several Mediterranean littoral states may acquire Chinese long-range precision guided missiles.[24] This means that the NATO Europe airfields may be subjected to missile bombardment during the early phases of any expeditionary operation.

---

[21] The British Army currently plans to defer its major AFV modernization program, the FRES project, until the end of the decade. See Chapter Two for further discussion of this issue. For a status report of the FRES program, see Christopher F. Foss, "Coming Together: A Year of Scout Work," *International Defense Review*, August 25, 2011; and Christopher Foss, "Scout SV-Representative Prototype Debuts," *Jane's Defense Weekly*, September 9, 2011.

[22] This is a good example of the consequence of shrinking force structure and budgets to the point where the armed forces in question have no reserve capacity once they are committed to a sustained power-projection mission.

[23] For a description of the precision-guided M600, also known as the Fateh-110 and the DF-11, see David Fulghum, "Israel Eyes M600 Ballistic Missile Threat," *Aviation Week and Space Technology*, August 9, 2011; and Naharnet Agencies, "Report: Hizbullah Deployed Syrian-Made Missile Capable of Destroying Israel," *World Council for the Cedars Revolution*, January 14, 2010.

[24] Not to be forgotten is the prospect that several littoral states may acquire an arsenal of long-range self-propelled mines. See Richard Scott, "ONR Seeks UUV Breakthroughs in Autonomy and Endurance," *International Defense Review*, August 5, 2011.

Even the NATO naval forces could be subject to both antiship cruise and ballistic missile attacks. This emerging threat points to the NATO Europe need for a robust strategic and tactical air and missile defense capability to protect both expeditionary forces as well as NATO bases from long-range precision attack. Unlike the threat of nuclear weapon use, the threat of long-range precision attack may be very credible, especially against those without adequate defenses.[25] Even more demanding would be a requirement to deploy a credible counterforce capability against this type of missile threat.[26] This is likely to be well beyond NATO Europe's capacity, much less that of the United States.

In conclusion, a Libyan-type scenario is the upper limit to any NATO Europe Mediterranean policing or intervention capability. Further, the potential forces listed above assume that Germany and Turkey will participate. In light of the two countries' reluctance to participate in the Libyan military operation, that is a very questionable assumption.

The Libyan operation demonstrated the difficulty of obtaining a NATO-wide consensus regarding a humanitarian intervention. In the future, any such intervention is likely to be a coalition operation involving some, but not all, NATO allies—perhaps without a formal NATO decision by the North Atlantic Council.

High-Intensity Power-Projection Missions in More-Distant Regions

Even more problematic is NATO Europe's capacity to conduct power-projection missions to more-distant regions, such as the Persian Gulf,

---

[25] The trend in NATO Europe is not favorable in this regard, with the likely cancellation of the ground-based MEADS terminal missile defense system and further cutbacks to the French, British, Italian, and German buy of next-generation theater missile defense–capable frigates. It is noteworthy that the threat of precision-guided SS-26 short-range ballistic missiles deployed by the Russian Federation in the Baltic region was cited by Swedish defense experts as an emerging military-technological problem.

[26] A NATO Europe capacity in this regard will be completely out of reach if the AGS system is canceled outright.

in the face of an even more severe regional military threat. Even if France and/or the UK were inclined to deploy a ground expeditionary force, after the planned cuts, each could at best provide one or two brigades to ports and/or airfields under U.S. and Gulf state air and missile defense protection.[27] As for the UK and French amphibious capabilities, it is highly unlikely that they would be deployed in a high-threat environment without considerable U.S. force protection.[28]

After the planned cuts, only France will be able to deploy a single CTOL-capable aircraft during this decade to support this type of contingency. The British and French hope to join forces with their carrier fleets by the early 2020s. By that time, the UK will have built two large STOVL carriers, the *Queen Elizabeth* and *Prince of Wales*. With the French *Charles de Gaulle* CTOL carrier, both nations hope to have a joint three-carrier fleet that will provide full-time readiness for at least one carrier to deal with rapidly emerging contingencies.[29]

However, the plan for a British-French three-carrier fleet assumes that the British will be to afford a fleet of high-performance STOVL fighter-bombers. Additionally, it is becoming increasingly clear that the Royal Navy will end up with only one new carrier, not two: As mentioned earlier, the British are planning to either "mothball" or sell one of their two new aircraft carriers, which would leave the combined Franco-British fleet with only two operational aircraft carriers.

A three-ship carrier fleet would allow the sustained presence of a single carrier or the more temporary surge deployment of two carriers with sufficient warning time. From the U.S. perspective, this would allow NATO Europe to provide a limited strike capability as part of

---

[27] In contrast to the current British and French ground force capacity, during Operation Desert Shield/Storm, France deployed a light motorized division and the UK deployed a heavy armored division. During Operation Iraqi Freedom, the UK deployed a division-sized task force of Army heavy brigades and Royal Marine amphibious commando battalions.

[28] Several French interviewees brought up the interesting prospect that France, and possibly the UK, might use these naval assets against the maritime interest of China in the event of major regional conflict involving China and the United States, as a show of strategic solidarity.

[29] The British F-35B will be able to operate off the CTOL-capable *Charles de Gaulle*, but the French Rafales will not be able to operate off the STOVL-only British carriers.

joint deterrent and/or combat capability during a future political military crisis with Iran. It is noteworthy that France will have a "theater" nuclear strike capability on board the *Charles de Gaulle* in the form of two squadrons of Rafale jet fighters, each capable carrying a nuclear-armed supersonic stand-off missile, the ASMP-B. There is currently no public plan for the Royal Navy to so arm its planned F-35B fleet, although the United States plans to provide a nuclear weapon delivery option for the F-35As that may be deployed in NATO Europe to maintain the current limited dual-key nuclear posture.

The NATO Europe forces would operate under the U.S. naval aerospace defense capability deployed during the crisis.[30] The only other rapidly deployable naval capability is the prospect that either or both France and the UK might deploy a small number of their SSNs armed with conventional cruise missiles to this theater of operation. This would be at best a token force, but has the benefit of being the most survivable of the power-projection options for France and the UK in this high-risk circumstance.

Long-Range Operations with Small "Conventional" Forces[31]

Even with the anticipated cuts, the naval forces of France, the UK, Germany, Italy, Spain, and others, such as Sweden and possibly the Netherlands, will be able support sustained counter-piracy operations in the Gulf of Aden region. It is unlikely that this naval capability will

---

[30] By the 2020s, the A2/AD capability of Iran may become quite formidable if supplied by China. The latter may have developed an arms-for-oil-and-gas arrangement with Iran similar to the U.S. and European strategic and economic posture toward Saudi Arabia.

[31] This analysis does not consider the requirement to maintain a multi-brigade capacity to support a distant big COIN operation, such as the current operation in Afghanistan. In light of that experience, NATO Europe has neither the will nor the capacity to maintain that type of robust peacekeeping operation capability. The new U.S. national military strategy makes it clear that the United States will avoid getting engaged in a future big COIN and nation-building operation, thereby justifying the decision for reducing the size of the U.S. Army and U.S. Marine Corps.

be employed in Asian counter-piracy operations, but the prospect of a policing operation off the coast of western Africa is not implausible.

As for more traditional peacekeeping operations in sub-Saharan Africa, France and the UK will retain brigade-sized airborne forces that could be airlifted to a distant peacekeeping operation. By the end of the decade, the NATO Europe airlift fleet will be a mix of over 100 operational A400Ms and a handful of UK and NATO C-17s. Additional C-130s and C-295s will be available as well.[32] This suggests that one or two BCT-sized forces could be sustained by NATO Europe airlift without U.S. airlift assistance.[33] Along the littoral of Africa, the UK, France, Spain, and Italy will retain an amphibious capability to support a single multinational brigade task force over very long distances for a multi-month operation. It is assumed that future military technological threats in these regions of Africa will have not matured in a meaningful way, although it is possible that at some point advanced man-portable air defense systems (MANPADS) and other ground-to-ground precision-guided weapons may have become available to the local military opposition, whether a state, a faction in a civil war, a terrorist group, or an independent militia.[34] As noted below, those forces, including those SOF units being used in support of a peacekeeping or foreign internal defense operation, will have to obtain tri-service transportation and combat vehicle assets equipped with increasingly sophisticated PGM and IED countermeasures.

After the planned cuts, the larger NATO European nations will be able to provide up to brigade-sized forces with some air support for protracted peace operations in locations such as sub-Saharan Africa. However, the reduced size of the European nations' armed forces means that such missions will represent considerably more strain to

---

[32] See Chapter Two for details.

[33] The UK hopes to have the capacity to conduct a single battalion parachute assault by mid-decade. Further reinforcement would arrive by airlift to an airfield seized by the airborne battalion. See Tim Ripley, "British Army Plans to Reactivate Airborne Task Force," *Jane's Defense Weekly*, August 25, 2011.

[34] As an example of this potential PGM diffusion phenomenon, see Lauren Gelfand, "Fears Rise over Ghadaffi Weapons 'Getting into Wrong Hands,'" *Jane's Defence Weekly*, September 9, 2011.

the Europeans than is the case today. Importantly, if the Europeans are already engaged in some other fairly large operation, they will be hard pressed to free forces for a peace operation in Africa. Similarly, if they are already engaged in an ongoing peace operation, it could compromise their ability to quickly respond to a new, unforeseen crisis.

Long-Range SOF Operations

In the past decade, the United States has encouraged its European allies to develop special operations forces, because of the strain on its own special operations forces. Several European militaries maintain very capable SOF-type organizations, such as the British SAS and the Italian San Marco naval commandos. These forces have proved to be very useful and capable in Iraq, Afghanistan, and elsewhere.[35]

During the past ten years of counterterrorism and COIN operations, members of NATO have developed a spectrum of highly trained and well-equipped special operations forces. Such forces are team-, platoon-, company-, and battalion-sized units with older (on average, compared with conventional ground forces) and very highly trained personnel. The most noteworthy equipment change in support of these forces has been the emergence of a family of UAVs that can provide persistent and optionally armed overhead surveillance.

Two main missions have emerged. The first is the direct support of small special operations forces during hostage-rescue situations or short-duration missions against high-value terrorist leadership targets. The second is the creation of a long-duration reconnaissance strike capability similar to Task Force Observe, Detect, Identify, and Neutralize (ODIN) in support of sustained foreign internal defense operations. Key members of NATO Europe, such as the UK, France, and

---

[35] Public reports suggest that France and the UK special forces, as well as other unspecified participants, have played a key role in advising and training the anti-Gaddafi forces. There are further reports suggesting the provision of forward CAS units. See Christopher Stephen, "Libya Conflict: British and French Soldiers Help Rebels Prepare Sirte Attack—Soldiers on the Ground in Eastern Libya Have Guided Bombers to Create Path for Opposition Fighters Toward Gaddafi's Birthplace," *The Guardian*, August 25, 2011.

Germany, have used their special operations forces extensively, especially during the ISAF mission in Afghanistan.[36]

All the other less-capable NATO Europe allies have similar capabilities, if only to provide a domestic counterterrorism capability. However, the NATO European powers have been slower to develop new indigenous capabilities in the realm of the full spectrum of UAVs, especially those that are armed. At present, the UK, Italy, and France have operated U.S. and Israeli unmanned combat air systems (UCASs) in support of their forces in Afghanistan.

The emergence of a robust NATO Europe UAV industry will depend largely on whether several bilateral or multilateral MALE and UCAS aerial systems are funded during this decade. At present, the jury is still out. An effort by France and the UK to jointly develop a MALE UAV that may have UCAS features appears to be making slow progress, largely due to lack of funding. An alternative program centered on Germany awaits a formal go-ahead.[37]

Left unresolved are the larger policy issues related to the Laws of Armed Conflict as to whether targeted "personalized" killings of terrorist and insurgent leaderships are legitimate forms of warfare in the name of national defense. The U.S. success in killing Osama bin Laden has highlighted a possible difference between the United States and its European allies in this regard.[38]

Thus, the issue for NATO Europe may have less to do with the availability of resources than whether several of the major European

---

[36] The UK SOF units were very active in their support of British units during Operation Iraqi Freedom.

[37] BAE Systems and Dassault Aviation plan to develop a MALE UAV known as the Telemos UAV. It will be developed with an armed or UCAS variant in mind. If robustly funded, this project will lead to an operational capability by the end of this decade. In potential competition is the EADS Cassidian unit that offers a similar UAV, the Talarion, with strong German, Spanish, and Turkish sponsorship. Both programs will be chasing limited European defense R&D funding. Adding to the mix is the active IAI armed version of the Hermes UAV. See Giovanni de Briganti, "BAE Systems–Dassault Aviation Telemos Prompts UAV Wars," defense-aerospace.com, June 16, 2011.

[38] Although the European governments either applauded or remained silent on the targeted killing of Osama bin Laden, there was a rather strong European media outcry denouncing this form of "personalized" warfare.

powers are prepared to conduct future counterterrorism operations that include personalized reconnaissance strike missions that rely on either human and/or robotic strike teams. At the present time, it appears that the UK, France, and Germany have answered this question in the affirmative. Certainly this form of warfare has many attractions, most notably the prospect that future failing or failed state interventions can avoid the deployment of traditional ground forces in protracted counterterrorism and foreign internal defense missions and the risk of attendant casualties.[39]

Similar to NATO Europe conducting future peacekeeping and/or foreign internal defense operations with conventional ground forces, future European sponsored SOF-type operations will have to take into account the diffusion of advanced MANPADS; light mobile air defenses; precision guided stand-off weapons in hands of terrorists; and high-performance criminal and/or insurgent organizations. However, future investment will have to be made in SOF transportation capabilities to make them less vulnerable to this diffusion of PGM technology.

Conclusion

When viewing NATO Europe's overall military capability in the coming decade, the lack of "quantity" has a qualitative effect. Given the anticipated cuts and future financial constraints, the capacity of the major European powers to project military power in the next decade will be highly constrained. Put simply, the units of account for European ground forces will be battalion battle groups and BCTs and not full-strength divisions and corps. The naval forces of the major European naval powers will radically shrink as well.

---

[39] This is not to say that SOF operations are inherently of low political and strategic risk. For example, the Carter administration suffered a heavy domestic and international loss after the failed Desert One hostage rescue operation in 1980. Its failure prompted the creation of U.S. Special Operations Command. The recent shoot-down of a CH-47G, with the loss of 30 American and 8 Afghan troops, in Afghanistan is a reminder of the risks of these types of operations. See Deb Riechmann, "Special Forces' Role Only to Grow, Missions Target Afghan Insurgents," *Boston Globe*, August 9, 2011.

In terms of NATO air power, if the RAF does not buy the F-35B, its resulting total inventory of 132 Typhoons by the end of the decade will mean that the RAF will be smaller than the air force of Singapore.

If UK and French forces were tied up in a protracted deployment along either the coast of African during a counter-piracy mission or while conducting a protracted peacekeeping operation in that continent's sub-Sahara region, their capacity to execute a time-urgent major Mediterranean expeditionary operation would be put under serious strain. Quite clearly, the employment of the joint British-French carrier battle group to the Persian Gulf region would significantly limit NATO Europe's immediate Mediterranean policing options, especially if the opponent could put NATO airfields at risk.

Conversely, if NATO Europe got involved in a major operation in the Mediterranean, it would likely not have any reserve capacity to address long-distance lower risk contingencies, much less a higher-risk contingency in the Persian Gulf region. At best, the United States can hope that NATO Europe, including France, the UK, Italy, and Spain, can maintain a militarily credible Mediterranean capacity, with the understanding of the limits of that capability.

CHAPTER FOUR

The Broader Strategic Context

As the preceding discussion underscores, in the coming decade, NATO Europe will face a new and very demanding security environment. It is not just that there will be less money for defense, but also that the strategic context is undergoing sharp changes that will complicate the security challenges NATO will face. These new challenges include the threat from transnational terrorism, the spread of weapons of mass destruction, threats from cyberspace, and threats posed by international criminal organizations.

These threats are emerging at a time when NATO Europe faces a very unpropitious economic environment that will impose sharp constraints on defense spending. Power projection outside of Europe's immediate neighborhood will be particularly difficult due to reduced force size, limited lift and logistics capability, and lack of certain key enablers (e.g., ISR, missile defense, UAVs).

The Limits of Smart Defense

Some NATO leaders suggest that the ambitious goals expressed in the Lisbon Ten list can be sustained through "smart defense" planning and programming. However, this approach has distinct limits. At best, it may lead to a rationalization of training, exercise, and logistics facilities. Hopes for major multinational European programs have fallen on hard times. An important example is the near death of the highly touted NATO Europe AGS ISR system. Denmark and Canada dropped out the program in the summer of 2011. The credibility of this joint program was further damaged by the German withdrawal of its crews from the NATO AWACS fleet during the opening stages of the NATO Libyan military operation.

France appears to be very skeptical of large multilateral programs undertaken in the name of cost sharing. French officials fear that France may be denied use of these programs during a future political-military crisis because one or more key partners could veto use of the systems due to political differences.[1] This has led to greater enthusiasm in Paris for bilateral developments with countries with similar "political strategic cultures"; this was a key rationale for the Franco-British treaty on military cooperation signed in November 2010.

Pooling and Sharing

As European governments have been forced to make deeper cuts in defense spending, they have begun to pay greater attention to the idea of pooling and sharing resources as a means of compensating for the impact of the cuts. The Dutch and Belgians, for instance, have agreed to naval training and maintenance. The Czechs and Slovaks are discussing sharing air force training, maintenance, logistics, and education; Slovenia and Croatia are contemplating building an integrated air force; and Denmark, Sweden, Finland, and Iceland have established the Nordic Defense Cooperation, which includes a joint center on the exchange of air traffic control data and more than 40 common procurement programs.

Pooling and sharing, however, is no panacea. It can help to rationalize defense efforts and reduce costs, but it cannot make up for sustained drops in defense spending. As Thomas Valasek has noted, European governments remain protective of their right to maintain and deploy their armed forces as they please. While they want to cut costs, many are hesitant to cede control when it comes to defense matters.[2]

---

[1] Discussions in Paris, July 20–21, 2011.

[2] Thomas Valasek, "Surviving Austerity," *Centre for European Reform*, April 2011, pp. 20–21.

Some states fear that if they merge part of their armed forces with another state, they will be pressured to participate in a mission because their pooling partner wants to take part regardless of whether it is in their interest to do so. Others have the opposite fear: that when they want to use a joint unit, they may be prevented from doing so by their partner. Finally, many states are concerned that pooling and sharing will lead to "free riding"—i.e., that poorer states will enjoy the benefits of pooling and sharing without contributing much themselves.

These attitudes are not likely to radically change in the next few years. Indeed, some may even be strengthened, depending on the outcome of the current financial crisis in Europe. Thus, U.S. and NATO officials will need to take these sensitivities into consideration in formulating future proposals for pooling and sharing efforts.

Other factors, such as a similar strategic culture, are also important. France and Germany were unable to use the Franco-German brigade in Afghanistan because of disagreements over where and with what caveats the brigade could be deployed. These disagreements are rooted in different national views on the degree of risk to which soldiers should be exposed.[3] For this reason, the Franco-British expeditionary force may have a better chance of success, since Britain and France share similar views about risk-taking in expeditionary operations. The integration of the Dutch and Belgian naval forces provides a good example of the benefits of pooling for smaller nations.

The Impact of the Euro Crisis

The defense challenges faced by the Alliance are exacerbated by the recession and sovereign debt crisis in Europe. The debt crisis has raised serious questions regarding the EU's future unity and ability to act as a strong, effective international actor. As *The Economist* has pointed out, "It is not just the euro that is at risk, but the future of the European Union and the world economy."[4] At every stage, European officials

---

[3] Discussions in Paris, July 20–21, 2011.

[4] "How to Save the Euro," *The Economist*, September 17, 2011.

have done just enough to avoid imminent collapse but not enough to establish a solid foundation for resolving the crisis. This has resulted in an unending series of crises that has eroded the confidence of investors and contributed to a climate of growing market volatility reminiscent of the 2008 crisis.

If the EU fails to manage the sovereign debt crisis more decisively, the Eurozone could collapse, crippling the global economic recovery and creating further pressures for defense cuts. The result would be a weaker, more fragmented EU. Under such circumstances, the incentive and impetus for greater coordination of defense policies would be significantly weakened. It would also be much harder to get member states to address many of the key challenges that the EU faces in the defense field. In short, the economic environment could further deteriorate, creating pressures for cutbacks in defense spending beyond those currently planned.

The European Defense Industrial Sector

The defense industrial sector in Europe is undergoing important changes. Austerity measures are forcing European aerospace and defense (A&D) companies to emphasize their global and multinational features to remain competitive in the global arms market. In the near term, arms sales outside of Europe will be given great emphasis.

The A&D industries of the United States and Europe will be increasingly in competition to find new business outside of their domestic national defense markets in the global arms market, especially in the more economically dynamic parts of South and East Asia. This phenomenon is especially true for the European A&D industries that face a steep downturn in NATO Europe's defense spending.

An example of this intra-European competition is EADS's attempt to underbid Dassault of France even after the latter "won" the competition to supply India with its Rafale fighter-bomber at the expense of EADS's Typhoon combat jet. Over the longer term, there is genuine concern that, without European national seed monies to invest in new-generation military technologies, even the big European multinational A&D companies will lose their independent competitive edge.[5]

Out of necessity, several companies, including BAE and EADS, have aggressively tried to expand their market share inside North America while making a major push in the global marketplace. In this regard, a number of European countries, especially France, may fight a rearguard effort to protect select A&D "national champions." However, that effort is likely to prove less and less financially feasible over time. In the spirit of multilateral bilateralism, the French are trying to expand their A&D ties with the UK while simultaneously attempting to develop similar ties with Germany in the field of naval warship building.

The Libyan Intervention: Lessons and Implications

Had they been asked in early 2011, few Western observers would have predicted that NATO would seek to militarily intervene in Libya. However, NATO's intervention in Libya is worth examining briefly for several reasons.

First, the intervention underscored that in the future the European members of NATO cannot automatically assume that the United States will always take the lead in every crisis. President Obama made clear that the United States was prepared to use its unique military assets in the initial stages of the conflict but that Washington expected the European members of the Alliance to take the main responsibility for the conduct of the military operation after that.

This does not mean that the United States will not get involved in future contingencies beyond Europe's borders. But in the future the United States will expect the European members of NATO to take more responsibility for managing crises in their immediate neighborhood.

The Libya campaign revealed progress in some areas. In the Kosovo conflict in 1999, the United States flew over 80 percent of the combat sorties. In Libya, by contrast, the majority of the sorties were

---

5 Discussions in Berlin, July 19, 2011.

flown by the European members of the Alliance, particularly France and Britain. As a result, the United States was able to take a public backseat and limit its military commitment.

However, the Libyan campaign exposed a number of operational and planning weaknesses that need to be addressed. Despite its overwhelming technological and numerical superiority against a fifth-rate military opponent, the coalition faced shortfalls in ammunition and weaponry in a number of areas. Many missions could not be carried out and sustained without significant U.S. military assistance. Without U.S. Tomahawk cruise missiles, drones, and electronic warfare aircraft to guide combat missions, the Libya intervention would have been extremely difficult and probably would not have succeeded.

In the future, the European allies need to pay greater attention to capabilities such as PGMs, surveillance, and refueling aircraft as well as UAVs. But finding the money to invest in these capabilities will prove difficult if many of the anticipated defense cuts are carried out.

Second, the Libyan campaign highlighted the importance of the use of special operations forces. NATO airpower was able to destroy much of Gaddafi's armor, artillery, and command and control infrastructure. NATO demonstrated the increasing efficacy of air-launched weapons, which the Alliance was able to use with minimal collateral damage.[6] At the same time, the campaign reaffirmed that airpower cannot by itself assure total victory. What proved to be critical in Libya was the deployment on the ground of special operations forces by Britain, France, and other nations (especially Qatar and the United Arab Emirates). These forces helped to arm and train the rebel forces and also coordinated CAS as rebel units advanced into Tripoli.[7]

The German decision not to participate in the Libyan operation caught many officials by surprise and raises questions about whether the Alliance can rely on Germany's support for future power-projection

---

6 As pointed out previously, the Libyan operation starkly demonstrated the military effectiveness of air forces supported by near-real-time ISR systems and armed with PGMs against mechanized forces that are without effective local, much less strategic, air defenses.

7 For a comprehensive study of the Libyan campaign, see the study by Adrian Johnson and Saqeb Mueen, *Short War, Long Shadow: The Political and Military Legacies of the 2011 Libyan Campaign*, London: Royal United Services Institute, Whitehall Report 1-12, 2012.

missions—even ones, like Libya, that are carried out under a UN mandate. In line with its decision not to participate in the Libyan operation, the German government removed its naval forces from the Mediterranean and withdrew its crews from the NATO AWACS.

German officials and experts acknowledge that the decision damaged Germany's standing in the Alliance. However, they contend that the decision was a "one-off" event prompted in large part by Chancellor Merkel's preoccupation with the Greek financial crisis, and that the decision should not be seen as an indication that Germany is embarking on a more independent security policy.[8]

While the current Bundeswehr reforms will improve the German Armed Forces' ability to conduct power-projection operations, the experience in Afghanistan has served to strengthen the German public's antipathy to involving German troops in foreign military interventions. Thus, getting Germany to take on a larger share of the security burden will not be easy. While Germany may be willing to participate in Alliance peacekeeping operations, it is likely to remain hesitant about using military force in a multinational context, even when it is sanctioned by a UN mandate.

Shifting U.S. Defense Priorities

These trends coincide with a shift in U.S. defense priorities. This shift is spelled out in the Obama administration's new national security strategy. The document calls for major changes in the size and orientation of the U.S. Army and U.S. Marine Corps and places special emphasis on the Asia Pacific region and the Middle East. It envisages the creation of a robust peacetime deterrent force with heavy reliance on modernizing air and naval forces to support a larger, multifaceted strategy to manage the rise of China as an emerging power.

In addition, the strategy calls for building a deterrent posture in the Persian Gulf region to deter a threat from an Iran that may acquire nuclear weapons in the not-too-distant future. Unlike the mili-

---

8 Steven Erlanger, "Libya's Dark Lesson for NATO," *New York Times*, September 3, 2011.

tary posture associated with U.S. Pacific Command's area of responsibility, U.S. Central Command's area of responsibility will require the peacetime deployment and possible employment of significant ground forces during a time of crisis and/or war. In this context, U.S. European Command will remain an important regional command in its own right while playing a major supporting role to U.S. Central Command's requirements to sustain a credible deterrent and warfighting posture in the Persian Gulf region.

As part of the strategy, the United States plans to withdraw two Army brigades and three USAF combat squadrons from Europe. This means that the United States will have only two brigades deployed in Europe. However, as the brigades to be withdrawn were deployed for long periods of time in Iraq and Afghanistan rather than in Europe, their removal will not result in a major loss of capability to protect Europe. At the same time, the United States plans to deploy four ballistic missile defense–capable Aegis ships at Naval Station Rota Spain, underscoring the administration's commitment to proceeding with the deployment of a NATO-wide missile defense system capable of protecting Europe against a potential ballistic missile threat from Iran.

This reorientation of U.S. strategy toward the Asia Pacific region does not mean that the United States is about to abandon Europe. American officials have gone out of their way to reassure America's European allies that "Europe is and remains America's partner of first resort."[9] But as the United States focuses more heavily on Asia in the coming decade, it will expect its European allies to take greater respon-

---

[9] See Secretary of State Hillary Clinton's remarks at the 2012 annual Munich Security Conference, February 4, 2012. Secretary of Defense Leon Panetta also sought to reassure the European allies that the U.S. focus on Asia would not result in a neglect of Europe, noting that "our military footprint in Europe will remain larger any other region in the world. That's not only because the peace and prosperity of Europe is critically important to the United States, but because Europe is our security partner, our security partner of choice for military operations and diplomacy around the world." See Leon Panetta, remarks at the 2012 Munich Security Conference, February 5, 2012. The joint appearance of Panetta and Clinton at the conference was a first and was designed to underscore that the United States would not abandon its European allies as it turned its attention toward the Asian Pacific region. See Elizabeth Bumuller and Steven Erlanger, "Panetta and Clinton Seek to Reassure Europe on Defense," *New York Times*, February 5, 2012.

sibility for managing crises in Europe and parts of its periphery. The United States will still be engaged politically and militarily in managing these crises, but it may not always take the lead in their management. Instead, it may play more of a backup role, as was the case in Libya.

CHAPTER FIVE

Implications and Recommendations for U.S. Policy

Financial and economic constraints are redefining NATO's ability to provide security in the coming decade. NATO faces more than a simple, short-term budget squeeze: It is confronted with a secular trend that will have a serious impact on NATO Europe's ability to deploy and sustain power over long distances.

As a result of the defense cuts under way, and those anticipated in the next several years, the air, land, and sea forces of key U.S. European allies are rapidly reaching the point where they can only perform one moderate-sized operation at a time and will be hard-pressed to meet the rotation requirements of a protracted, small-scale irregular warfare mission.

Power projection and sustainment of significant forces outside of Europe's immediate neighborhood will be particularly difficult due to reduced force size, limited lift and logistics capability, and lack of certain key enablers (e.g., ISR, missile defense, UAVs). Additionally, several key NATO European nations are either eliminating or significantly reducing key capabilities, such as littoral maritime forces and the related ISR platforms.

Transatlantic Defense Challenges in an Era of Austerity

In light of the cuts currently under way and those that are anticipated, maintaining a viable Alliance defense posture that can ensure peace and security in the coming decade will pose a formidable challenge. Alliance members will have to find ways to provide security with fewer resources. A number of measures, discussed below, would help to strengthen NATO's ability to meet this challenge.

Pooling and Sharing. As European governments have been forced to make deeper cuts in defense spending, they have begun to pay greater attention to the idea of pooling and sharing resources as a means of compensating for the impact of the cuts. However, while pooling and sharing can help to rationalize defense efforts and reduce costs, it cannot make up for sustained drops in defense spending. Bilateral partnerships, such as the British-French Defense Co-operation Treaty, may provide a more effective way of reducing costs and producing synergies and should be encouraged.

Leapfrogging. The strategy of "leapfrogging"—cutting defense expenditures heavily today while investing in new types of capabilities—may also prove to be a more effective way of coping with changing technological realities, emerging new threats, and declining defense budgets than maintaining the old capabilities. Specifically, the question at hand is whether NATO Europe is prepared to sustain even a minimum investment in new capabilities, such as high-performance ISR platforms, missile defense, advanced PGMs, unmanned vehicles, and robust cyber capabilities to ensure that a leapfrogging strategy is not just a leap-down strategy of more complete long-term disarmament.

Informal Ad Hoc Coalitions. As the Libyan intervention underscored, in the future, internal differences within the Alliance regarding threat perceptions and willingness to use force may make it difficult to obtain a consensus for NATO to engage in some missions beyond Europe's borders. As a result, we are likely to see coalitions of allies operating outside a NATO context, as Britain, France, the United Arab Emirates, and Qatar did on the ground in Libya, even as they participated with the NATO-led efforts in the air. This highlights the importance of sustaining interoperability among U.S. forces and the forces of individual NATO allies. This, in turn, requires maintaining a U.S. force posture in Europe that can be augmented in time of crisis and will require regular training and exercise missions with U.S. forces based in the United States.

British-French Defense Cooperation. The United States should encourage Britain and France to intensify the defense cooperation that they initiated with the signing of the November 2010 defense treaty. As noted, this bilateral agreement is important to the effort by Britain and France to maintain a carrier fleet that could assist the United States during any future containment strategy in response to Iran's assertion of regional hegemony. Britain's firm engagement in Europe is critical to maintaining NATO's political and military vitality in the coming decade and should be strongly encouraged by Washington. Without strong British participation, it will be difficult to build a strong European defense identity within NATO.

Crisis Management in the Maghreb. Washington should encourage NATO Europe to take lead responsibility for managing crises in the Maghreb[1]—a region in which Europe, especially the southern Alliance members, have a strong historical interest. In this region, the United States would play a supporting role, providing key enablers to European allies that would have the lead in day-to-day military missions.

As part of this new division of labor, the United States should encourage France, the UK, and Italy, together with Spain, to assume primary responsibility for ensuring peace and stability in the Maghreb and to maintain forces capable of carrying out this task. In particular, the United States should encourage the French and British to widen the scope of their military cooperation to include closer integration of their military forces with Italy and Spain.

The Weimar Triangle and Baltic Region. In addition, Germany should be encouraged to take on greater responsibility for ensuring security and stability in Eastern Europe. The United States should urge Germany to maintain a robust ground force for this purpose. At the same time, Berlin should be encouraged to intensify defense cooperation with Poland within the framework of the Weimar Triangle and to work closely with Denmark and Sweden to ensure the security of the Baltic region. In addition, defense cooperation between NATO and Sweden and Finland should be strengthened.

---

[1] The Maghreb refers to the area West of Egypt and includes Morocco, Tunisia, Algeria, Libya, and Mauritania.

Sustaining the Alliance over the Long Run

As the United States focuses more on Asia in the coming decade, Europe and NATO may become less central in U.S. strategy than they have been in the past. However, U.S. officials should be careful not to throw the baby out with the bathwater. The Cold War may be over, but NATO continues to serve a number of important security functions.

First, the Alliance serves as the primary framework for coordinating transatlantic security cooperation. This function is particularly important at a time when the EU is facing a major political and financial crisis that has slowed—and could possibly derail—the process of European integration and cooperation.

Second, NATO Europe plays an important role in maintaining key infrastructure and lines of communications to sustain a U.S.-led containment strategy in the Greater Middle East.

Third, NATO helps to reduce defense duplication and prevent the renationalization of defense. Without NATO, the individual Alliance members would be forced to spend considerably more money on defense than they currently do.

Fourth, NATO provides an important mechanism for managing the nuclear issue and coordinating Western nuclear policy. This function is likely to become more important in the future, given the uncertainties surrounding Iran's nuclear policy.

Fifth, NATO provides an insurance policy against the emergence of a resurgent Russia. This is particularly important for the new members from Central and Eastern Europe, who remain concerned that Russia, once it has recovered from the weakness and turmoil evident after the collapse of the Soviet Union, could once again pose a threat to its smaller, less-powerful neighbors.

Thus, there remain strong reasons for maintaining a vital NATO alliance capable of addressing threats to security in areas beyond Asia.

What does all this mean for the United States and NATO? It is important for the United States and the European members of NATO to candidly recognize that the nature and magnitude of the upcoming defense cuts in NATO Europe are significant, very significant. America's European allies are in the process of making major reductions in their military capabilities. Arguing for smart defense or pooling and sharing is fine, but it does not change the fundamental reality that the United States' NATO allies will, by the mid-2010s, have much less military capability than they do in 2012. Indeed, the ability of the European members of NATO to guarantee their own security in the immediate vicinity of Europe, much less in areas farther afield where their interests might be threatened, such as in the Greater Middle East, is rapidly eroding. To protect their own interests, as well as to give the United States some degree of reassurance that NATO Europe is not becoming dependent on the United States to a dangerously unprecedented extent, the European members of the Alliance will have to arrest the sharp downward spiral of their defense capabilities. NATO has been a major force of stability in the world for nearly seven decades. In order for NATO to retain its political and military relevance, the current course that many of its member states are on will have to change.

Bibliography

"A Happy Union?" *Jane's Defense Weekly*, August 11, 2011.

Adamowski, Jaroslaw, "Poland's Defense Budget Rises, with Emphasis on Modernization," *Defense News*, September 20, 2010.

"Aircraft Carriers: NAO Fear over Defence Review Change," *BBC News Online*, July 7, 2011.

"Air Force—France," *Jane's World Air Forces*, July 27, 2011.

"Air Force—Germany," *Jane's World Air Forces*, May 6, 2011.

"Air Force—Spain," *Jane's World Air Forces*, March 21, 2011.

"Air Force—Spain," *Jane's World Air Forces*, August 12, 2011.

"Army 2020: Presentation to the Army Chain of Command 5 July 2012," Secretary of State A2020 announcement, UK Ministry of Defence, 2012.

"Army—France," *Jane's World Armies*, July 12, 2011.

"Army—Germany," *Jane's World Armies*, July 22, 2011.

"Army—Spain," *Jane's World Armies*, March 7, 2011.

Ballantyne, Iain, "The Great Transition: New Royal Navy Abandons Primacy in Maritime Domain," *Defense IQ*, October 27, 2010.

Bayley, Hugh, "Information Document: The Global Financial Crisis and Its Impact on Defense Budgets," 2009 Annual Session Reports, NATO Parliamentary Assembly, November 2009.

Barnes, Julian E., "U.S. to Cut Europe Forces in Remake," *Wall Street Journal*, February 17, 2012.

Benitz, Jorge, "Impact of German Defense Cuts on Force Structure and Procurement Decisions," *NATO Source*, December 14, 2010.

"British Military to Follow US Example of Smaller Armed Forces," *Eurasia Review*, February 6, 2012.

Brune, Sophie, Alistair Cameron, Jean-Pierre Maulny, and Marcin Terlikowski, "Restructuring Europe's Armed Forces in Times of Austerity: The United Kingdom, France, Germany and Poland," Working Paper—Stiftung Wissenschaft und Politik, November 2010.

Bumuller, Elizabeth, and Steven Erlanger, "Panetta and Clinton Seek to Reassure Europe on Defense," *New York Times*, February 5, 2012.

"Cameron to Discuss Carrier Sharing Deal," *Defence Management*, October 28, 2010.

Carr, Jeffrey, "What Is Cyberwar? The Defense Community Can't Figure Out How to Define It," *Slate*, August 12, 2011.

"Central Europe and the Baltic States—Armed Forces—Poland," *Jane's Sentinel Security Assessment*, August 23, 2011.

"Central Europe and the Baltic States—Army—Poland," *Jane's Sentinel Security Assessment*, August 23, 2011.

"Central Europe and the Baltic States—Navy—Poland," *Jane's Sentinel Security Assessment*, October 26, 2011.

"Central Europe and the Baltic States—Procurement—Poland," *Jane's Sentinel Security Assessment*, November 4, 2011.

Chuter, Andrew, "UK to Up Equipment Funds, Cut Active Duty Troops," *Defense News*, July 18, 2011.

Clinton, Hillary, remarks at the 2012 Munich Security Conference, February 4, 2012. As of March 9, 2012:
http://www.securityconference.de/Hillary-R-Clinton.827+M52087573ab0.0.html

Contigugulia, Cat, "ČR, Poland Talk Military Alliance: Top Generals Convene Meeting on Pooling of Resources amid Cuts," *Prague Post*, October 19, 2011.

Daalder, Ivo, and James Stavridis, "NATO's Victory in Libya: The Right Way to Run an Intervention," *Foreign Affairs*, Vol. 91, No. 2, March/April 2012, pp. 2–7.

Day, Matthew, "Poland Ends Army Conscription," *Daily Telegraph*, August 5, 2008.

de Briganti, Giovanni, "BAE Systems–Dassault Aviation Telemos Prompts UAV Wars," defense-aerospace.com, June 16, 2011.

"Défense et Sécurité Nationale: Le Livre Blanc," Odile Jacob/La Documentation Francaise, Paris, June 2008

Dempsey, Judy, "German Committee Recommends Cutbacks in Defense Spending," *New York Times*, October 24, 2010.

"Dutch Initiate Defense Cuts," *Defense Technology International*, June 1, 2011.

Erlanger, Steven, "Libya's Dark Lesson for NATO," *New York Times*, September 3, 2011.

European Parliament, Policy Department, Directorate-General for External Policies, *The Impact of the Financial Crisis on European Defence: Annex*, Brusssels, 2011.

"Fact Sheet: U.S.-Poland Bilateral Defense Cooperation," Office of the Press Secretary, The White House, May 28, 2011.

Fidler, Steven, "Cutting Defense Around Europe," *WSJ Blogs: Real Time Brussels*, June 25, 2010. As of March 9, 2012:
http://blogs.wsj.com/brussels/2010/06/25/cutrting-defense-around-europe/

Flanagan, Stephen F., Guy Ben-Ari, David J. Berteau, Heather A. Conley, Joachim Hofbauer, T. J. Cipoletti, Roy Levy, and Alessandro Scheffler, "A Diminishing Transatlantic Partnership?" Washington, D.C.: Center for Strategic and International Studies, May 2011.

Foss, Christopher F., "Coming Together: A Year of Scout Work," *International Defense Review*, August 25, 2011.

———, "Scout SV-Representative Prototype Debuts," *Jane's Defense Weekly*, September 9, 2011.

"The French White Paper on Defence and National Security," 2008.

Fulghum, David, "Israel Eyes M600 Ballistic Missile Threat," *Aviation Week and Space Technology*, August 9, 2011.

Gelfand, Lauren, "Fears Rise over Ghadaffi Weapons 'Getting into Wrong Hands,'" *Jane's Defence Weekly*, September 9, 2011.

Geramone, Jim, "U.S., Poland Sign Special Ops Memo of Understanding," American Foreign Press Service, February 19, 2009.

"Germany Builds Future Beyond EU," *International Herald Tribune*, July 19, 2011.

"How to Save the Euro," *The Economist*, September 17, 2011.

Hugemark, Bo, *Friends in Need: Toward a Swedish Strategy of Solidarity with Her Neighbours*, Stockholm: Royal Swedish Academy of War Science, 2012.

Hughes, Robin, "North Korea Aiding Syria to Upgrade Scud D Capability," *International Defence Review*, June 26, 2012.

The Impact of the Financial Crisis on European Defence: Annex—*See* European Parliament, Policy Department, Directorate-General for External Policies, *The Impact of the Financial Crisis on European Defence: Annex*, Brusssels, 2011.

Ing, David, "Spanish Defence Spending Down 50 Per Cent Since 2008," *Jane's Defence Weekly*, July 6, 2011.

"Iran's Ballistic Missile Capabilities—A Net Assessment," *IISS Strategic Dossier*, London: The International Institute for Strategic Studies, 2010.

Johnson, Adrian, and Saqeb Mueen, *Short War, Long Shadow: The Political and Military Legacies of the 2011 Libyan Campaign*, London: Royal United Services Institute, Whitehall Report 1-12, 2012.

Jones, Gregory S., "An In-Depth Examination of Iran's Centrifuge Enrichment Program and Its Efforts to Acquire Nuclear Weapons," *Nonproliferation Policy Education Center*, August 9, 2011.

Keller, Patrick, "Challenges for European Defense Budgets After the Economic Crisis," *AEI*, July 2011, p. 3.

Lekic, Slobodan, "5 Polish Troops Killed by Bomb in East Afghanistan," *Associated Press*, December 21, 2011.

Lehrke, Dylan Lee, "Deterrent Dilemma—UK Examines Its Nuclear Options," *Jane's Intelligence Review*, July 10, 2012.

"Liam Fox Announces Army Cuts but Promises Extra Funds in the Future," *The Guardian*, July 18, 2011.

"Libyan War 'Puts Britain's Defence at Risk:' First Sea Lord Warns That Conflict Can Only Last Another 90 Days," *The Daily Mail*, June 14, 2011.

"Lord Dannatt's Warning About Army Cuts," *British Forces News*, May 11, 2011.

Mackenzie, Christina, and Andy Nativi, "Chopping Budgets in Europe," *Aviation Week*, January 5, 2012.

"Military Experts' Warning over Defense Spending Review," *The Telegraph*, January 29, 2011.

"MoD Sacrifices Manpower to Pay for Equipment," *The Telegraph*, July 19, 2011.

Mölling, Christian, and Sophie-Charlotte Brune, *The Impact of the Financial Crisis on European Defence*, Brussels: Directorate-General for External Policies of the Union—Policy Department, European Parliament, Ref: EP/EXPO/B/SEDE/FWC/2009-01/Lot6/09, April 2011.

Naharnet Agencies, "Report: Hizbullah Deployed Syrian-Made Missile Capable of Destroying Israel," *World Council for the Cedars Revolution*, January 14, 2010.

Narodowej, Ministerstwo Obrony, "Podstawowe Informacje o Budzecie Resotru Obrony Narodowej na 2012 R," Department Budzetowy, Warsawa, Marzec, 2012 R.

"NATO 2020: Assured Security; Dynamic Engagement—Analysis and Recommendations of the Group of Experts on a New Strategic Concept for NATO," NATO Public Diplomacy Division, May 17, 2010, written in preparation for the NATO Summit at Lisbon, November 2010.

"NATO Defence Planning Capability Review 2010/11," NATO Defence Policy and Planning Committee (Reinforced), Working Paper AC/281-WP 0049 (R), 2011.

"NATO Semestrial Statistical Memorandum," 2011.

"Navy—France," *Jane's World Navies*, August 2, 2011.

"Navy—Germany," *Jane's World Navies*, July 22, 2011.

Nicol, David C., "Hacking the Lights Out: Computer Viruses Have Taken Out Hardened Industrial Control Systems—The Electric Power Grid May Be Next," *Scientific American*, July 2011.

"NL Defense Post-Financial Crisis," *Defensie Afdeling*, August 11, 2011.

Odile, Jacob, "Défense et Sécurité Nationale: Le Livre Blanc," *La Documentation Francaise*, Paris, June 2008, p. 211.

Oliker, Olga, Keith Crane, Lowell H. Schwartz, and Catherine Yusupov, *Russian Foreign Policy Sources and Implications*, Santa Monica, Calif.: RAND Corporation, MG-768-AF, 2009. As of March 9, 2012:
http://www.rand.org/pubs/monographs/MG768.html

Office of the Under Secretary of Defense (Comptroller)/Chief Financial Officer, *Overview, Fiscal Year 2013 Budget Request*, Washington, D.C., February 2012.

Panetta, Leon, remarks at the 2012 Munich Security Conference, February 5, 2012. As of March 9, 2012:
http://www.securityconference.de/Leon-Panetta.828+M544261a91d7.0.html

Rasmussen, Anders Fogh, "NATO After Libya," *Foreign Affairs*, Vol. 90, No. 4, July/August 2011, p. 3.

"Recent Defense Spending Plans Announced by EU Member States," *Europolitics*, November 30, 2010.

Riechmann, Deb, "Special Forces' Role Only to Grow, Missions Target Afghan Insurgents," *Boston Globe*, August 9, 2011.

Ripley, Tim, "British Army Plans to Reactivate Airborne Task Force," *Jane's Defense Weekly*, August 25, 2011.

Rosamond, Jon, "Europe Takes the Strain on Operation 'United Protector,'" *Jane's Navy International*, July/August 2011.

Scott, Richard, "ONR Seeks UUV Breakthroughs in Autonomy and Endurance," *International Defense Review*, August 5, 2011.

"Showing the Strain," *The Economist*, July 14, 2011.

"SM-3 Antimissile System Receives Key Backing at Pentagon," *Global Security Newswire*, August 8, 2011.

"Spain," *The Military Balance*, London: International Institute for Strategic Studies, September 20, 2011.

"Spain Makes New Vehicle Order," *Jane's Defence Weekly*, September 12, 2011.

"Spain Won't Reduce Budget for Afghanistan's Military Mission—Min. Chacon," *Kuwait News Agency (KUNA)*, June 21, 2011.

Stephen, Christopher, "Libya Conflict: British and French Soldiers Help Rebels Prepare Sirte Attack—Soldiers on the Ground in Eastern Libya Have Guided Bombers to Create Path for Opposition Fighters Toward Gaddafi's Birthplace," *The Guardian*, August 25, 2011.

———, "French, UK Special Operations Clear Path for Rebel Forces Attack on Sirte," *The Irish Times*, August 28, 2011.

"Sustaining U.S. Global Leadership: Priorities for 21st Century Defense," U.S. Department of Defense, January 2012.

Sweetman, Bill, "Under Fire—Navy Study Looks at Killing One Joint Strike Fighter Version," *Aviation Week & Space Technology*, August 29, 2011.

Tan, Michelle, and Richard Sandza, "European Pullout Plan to Move 2 BCTs and up to 10,000 Soldiers Could Start in October," *Army Times*, January 23, 2012.

"The Netherlands Defence Organisation After the Credit Crunch: A Smaller Force in a Troubled World," April 19, 2011, memorandum provided to RAND by Royal Netherlands Embassy on July 13, 2011.

Thornton, Rod, *Military Modernization and the Russian Ground Forces*, Carlisle, Pa.: Strategic Studies Institute, 2011.

"UK Defense Ministry Looks to Further Cuts," *Jane's Intelligence Weekly*, January 20, 2011.

"UK Forces Braced for Deeper Cuts," *Jane's Defense Weekly*, June 17, 2011.

U.S. Department of State, Bureau of European and Eurasian Affairs, "Background Notes—Poland," August 30, 2011.

Valasek, Thomas, "Surviving Austerity," *Centre for European Reform*, April 2011, pp. 20–21.

Valpolini, Paolo, "Italy Cuts Funding for Libyan Operations," *Jane's Defense Weekly*, July 8, 2011.

Wasserbly, Daniel, "US Looks to Salvage MEADS Components," *International Defense Review*, August 25, 2011.

"Western Europe—Air Force—Italy," *Jane's Sentinel Security Assessment*, March 22, 2011.

"Western Europe—Air Force—Netherlands, *Jane's Sentinel Security Assessment*, June 17, 2011.

"Western Europe—Armed Forces—Italy," *Jane's Sentinel Security Assessment*, April 14, 2011.

"Western Europe—Armed Forces—Germany," *Jane's Sentinel Security Assessment*, July 22, 2011.

"Western Europe—Armed Forces—Netherlands," *Jane's Sentinel Security Assessment*, June 13, 2011.

"Western Europe—Armed Forces—Spain," *Jane's Sentinel Security Assessment*, March 7, 2011.

"Western Europe—Armed Forces—United Kingdom," *Jane's Sentinel Security Assessment*, August 24, 2011.

"Western Europe—Army—Italy," *Jane's Sentinel Security Assessment*, April 14, 2011.

"Western Europe—Army—Spain," *Jane's Sentinel Security Assessment*, March 7, 2011.

"Western Europe—Army—Netherlands," *Jane's Sentinel Security Assessment*, June 13, 2011.

"Western Europe—Defense Budget Overview—France," *Jane's Sentinel Security Assessment*, March 4, 2011.

"Western Europe—Defense Budget Overview—Italy," *Jane's Sentinel Security Assessment*, April 14, 2011.

"Western Europe—Navy—Italy," *Jane's Sentinel Security Assessment*, April 14, 2011.

"Western Europe—Navy—Netherlands," *Jane's Sentinel Security Assessment*, June 13, 2011.

"Western Europe—Navy—Spain," *Jane's Sentinel Security Assessment*, May 19, 2011.

"Western Europe—Navy—United Kingdom," *Jane's Sentinel Security Assessment*, June 30, 2011.

"Western Europe—Procurement—Germany," *Jane's Sentinel Security Assessment*, July 22, 2011.

"Western Europe—Procurement—Netherlands," *Jane's Sentinel Security Assessment*, June 17, 2011.

"Western Europe—Procurement—United Kingdom," *Jane's Sentinel Security Assessment*, July 4, 2011.

"World Armies—Poland," *Jane's World Armies*, December 19, 2011.